Day to Day the Relationship Way

Creating Responsive Programs for Infants & Toddlers

Donna S. Wittmer & Alice Sterling Honig

National Association for the Education of Young Children
Washington DC

National Association for the
Education of Young Children
1313 L Street NW, Suite 500
Washington, DC 20005-4101
202-232-8777 • 800-424-2460
NAEYC.org

NAEYC Books

Senior Director, Publishing
and Professional Learning
Susan Friedman

Director, Books
Dana Battaglia

Senior Editor
Holly Bohart

Editor
Rossella Procopio

Senior Creative Design Manager
Henrique J. Siblesz

Senior Creative Design Specialist
Charity Coleman

Senior Creative Design Specialist
Gillian Frank

Publishing Business
Operations Manager
Francine Markowitz

Through its publications program,
the National Association
for the Education of Young
Children (NAEYC) provides a
forum for discussion of major
issues and ideas in the early
childhood field, with the hope
of provoking thought and
promoting professional growth.
The views expressed or implied
in this book are not necessarily
those of the Association.

Photo Credits

© Michael Harrison: cover

© Getty Images: 2, 5, 10, 11, 12, 18, 20, 21, 25, 27,
31, 35, 39, 40, 45, 47, 49, 51, 53, 56, 58, 60, 68,
70, 73, 80, 83, 87, 90, 99, 102, 119, 122, 123, 134,
and 141

Courtesy of Donna S. Wittmer: 107 and 109

Contents

Introduction

A baby's smile can make you simply melt. Observing as infants (birth to 1 year) develop into young toddlers (1–2 years), and then older toddlers (2–3 years), you marvel at how they change so rapidly and learn so quickly. You appreciate their incredible curiosity about things that you might not notice as much anymore—a flower, a bug, or water flowing down a sidewalk.

Teachers of children birth to 3 play many roles, including educator, caregiver, child development specialist, facilitator of learning, program creator, and relationship builder with children and families. One of the most important roles is to help infants and toddlers develop a healthy sense of self and experience caring relationships with adults and their peers. By understanding young children as individuals, protecting them, cherishing them, encouraging them, and helping them learn, you help give them a wonderful start in life.

Who Are Teachers?

In this book we refer to professionals who work with children from birth to 3 and their families in their homes, center programs, family child care homes, or other settings as *teachers*.

Relationship-Based, Responsive Programs for Infants and Toddlers

A relationship-based approach to responsive programs for young children emphasizes the importance of consistent, respectful, and affectionate relationships—adult–child, teacher–family, and between peers—for children's development and learning (Degotardi, Page, & White 2017; Lally & Mangione 2017). Genuinely caring for a child's well-being promotes a harmonious connection with you and with other adults and peers in the program and supports the child's feeling of being secure in your presence.

This emphasis on developing a trusting bond with children and families guides your decisions about how to meet children's needs and organize your program. The relationship-based philosophy for being and working with infants and toddlers that is described in this book includes the following 10 important elements that guide teachers' thinking about young children and their needs.

Early Loving and Learning Experiences Matter

From birth, young children are capable and eager to learn. When infants and toddlers feel secure and loved, they are much more likely to develop warm relationships with others and engage fully in learning experiences (Birmingham, Bub, & Vaughan 2017; Boldt et al. 2014; Ebbeck, Warrier, & Goh 2018; Groh et al. 2014). They need many enriching opportunities to learn in a program that is appropriate for their ages, individual development, personalities, and family cultures.

These early experiences matter for children's healthy brain growth. While genes play an important role in forming basic brain architecture, experiences before birth and in the first few years of life are key to shaping continued brain development (Center on the Developing Child, n.d. a; Zero to Three, n.d.). Young children learn best when the important adults in their lives keep them safe, are responsive to their needs, cuddle and comfort them, talk and sing with them, and provide a variety of learning opportunities.

Young children's brain development is also vulnerable to negative experiences. Toxic stress, trauma, neglect, and child abuse can negatively affect brain development and children's present and future health (Bick et al. 2015; CDC 2020). Children who experience child abuse and neglect before the age of 5, for example, are more challenged socially and academically as they grow older (Raby et al. 2018; Rokita, Dauvermann, & Donohoe 2018).

Infants and Toddlers Need Loving, Consistent Relationships

Feeling that they are valued, respected, and treasured enables young children to develop satisfying and fulfilling emotional connections with their families, teachers, and peers. These positive relationships provide a foundation for future relationships and for learning (Degotardi 2017; Degotardi, Page, & White 2017; Ebbeck et al. 2015; Owen et al. 2008; Sosinsky et al. 2016).

Infants and toddlers exist within a network of relationships with families, teachers, peers, and communities. Those in the network interact with and influence each other as well as the child (Bronfenbrenner 2005). Children benefit when you respect the power of a child's network of relationships and recognize the importance of working with these layers of relationships.

Caring, Responsive Adults Help Infants and Toddlers Thrive

A teacher's warm responsiveness involves the ability to read a child's nonverbal and verbal cues for what she needs and enjoys and then to sensitively meet the child's physical, emotional, and learning needs (Mesman, Minter, & Angnged 2016; Mortensen & Barnett 2015). Responsiveness with young children involves reciprocity—engaging with infants and toddlers in a way that encourages them to be active participants in interactions. You build on young children's curiosity, desire to experiment, and motivation to learn. You facilitate learning by providing experiences and then engaging in responsive ways with language, encouragement, compassion, or your quiet presence. Your ability to read children's cues and respond in an affectionate way encourages problem solving, boosting children's emotional satisfaction and learning. You understand "the richness of everyday moments" (Mitchelmore, Degotardi, & Fleet 2017, 87). This means that each experience with a child, such as babbling back and forth with an older infant, has the potential to fulfill the child's profound need for satisfying interactions with you.

Children Deserve Respect as Persons with Feelings, Thoughts, and Rights

The United Nations created the Convention on the Rights of the Child to highlight the rights children have, including the right to survival; to develop to the fullest; to protection from harmful influences, abuse, and exploitation; and to participate fully in family, cultural, and social life. The four core principles are "non-discrimination, devotion to the best interests of the child; the right to life, survival and development; and respect for the views of the child" (CRC, n.d.). Each day, you recognize the rights of infants and toddlers when you respect that they are persons with feelings, desires, and needs that deserve your thoughtful attention and you support their participation in engaged learning.

Children Are Active, Capable Learners

Young children search for meaning in all that they do. For example, Diego, a young toddler, intently investigates a toy car by turning it over, running its wheels on the ground, shaking it softly and then more vigorously, tasting it, spinning the wheels, and throwing it. Through this exploration and similar ones, Diego is extending his understanding of gravity, how objects fit in space, and cause-and-effect relationships—and he learns that some objects do not taste good! Diego also is exposed to new language when his teacher says, "You turned the little car over. You're spinning the wheels."

From experiential learning like this, infants and toddlers develop *schemas*, or ideas about objects and people (Piaget 1968). They develop expectations about how materials, toys, and equipment work. When you are observant and responsive, you can provide young children with learning opportunities that build on their motivation to experience the world around them.

Successful Social and Emotional Development Are Critical to Learning

Healthy social and emotional experiences during the first three years of life *enable* brain growth, while stressful experiences such as persistent fear, stress, anxiety, and neglect *prevent* optimal brain development (NSCDC 2010, 2014). Infants' and toddlers' growing abilities to manage their emotions, understand others' emotions, and navigate social interactions influence their cognitive, language, and motor development both now and in the future (Hymel & Ford 2014).

Responsive Teachers Recognize the Uniqueness in Each Child

Teaching is a process of knowing each child personally—what excites him, his moods, and his needs—and what makes him happy, upset, or content. Responsive teachers provide developmentally appropriate experiences that are age, individually, and culturally appropriate (NAEYC 2018). Teachers figure out by observing each individual child what sparks his learning and loving strengths and needs.

Infants and Toddlers Live and Learn in Families and Communities

Communities and public policies affect the quality of families' lives (Bronfenbrenner 2005), which in turn influence the quality of young children's lives. To help infants and toddlers thrive, you must think about all the varied influences on their lives. It is crucial to support policies and laws that are family friendly and support quality in programs for infants and toddlers.

Loving and Learning Occur Within a Context

Children's experiences influence their development, behavior, and thinking (Vygotsky 1978). Family cultures, values, and practices affect children's attitudes about others, what is important to learn, and how to learn. To provide thoughtful, responsive care and education for young children, you must continually reflect on individual, family, and cultural factors. In addition, it is essential that you reflect on how your own biases about children's identities (race, gender, and culture, for example) might influence your work with children (Maclaughlin 2017).

Your Work Is Both Joyful and Challenging

While being with young children from day to day brings deep satisfaction, it sometimes tests the resolve of even the most caring and knowledgeable teacher! This book is intended to support you in making a challenging job easier and more fulfilling. You make a significant difference in the lives of children and families and thus deserve the utmost respect.

Whether your work with young children takes place in a center-based learning program, a family child care program, an early intervention program, a family-centered home visiting program, or other early learning setting, your professional passion is to help infants and toddlers thrive. The positive relationships that you develop with the children and families in your program and the knowledge, skills, and attitudes that children learn with you will affect them for many years. Although they may not remember your name several years from now, you become a part of who *they* will become. Together with families, you are a keeper and supporter of the essence of each child.

PART 1

Meeting Young Children's Needs Through Strong Relationships

At the heart of programs that effectively nurture infants' and toddlers' development and learning are relationships—relationships between children and families, children and teachers, peers, and families and teachers. Part 1 explores this important foundation. Chapter 1 emphasizes why relationships are so critical for young children's health and well-being and how to develop these relationships during your daily interactions with children. In Chapter 2, you will discover ways to develop responsive relationships with children's families and support children's relationships with their families.

Chapter 1

Build Strong Relationships with Infants and Toddlers

Infants and toddlers in thriving relationships with special adults feel safe, protected, appreciated, and loved. When an infant establishes a relationship with a sensitive and responsive caregiver, the infant learns whom to trust and turn to when needing support (Howes & Spieker 2008). Children use adults as secure bases from which to explore their world and to return to when they need to feel safe or desire food, attention, or a hug (Kaplan 1978; Vaughn et al. 2016). Young children who experience secure relationships are happier, kinder, more social, less anxious, and better learners than those children who do not feel secure (Brumariu & Kerns 2013; Groh et al. 2014; Panfile & Laible 2012).

Infants and toddlers show that they are developing secure and close, caring relationships with their teachers in many ways (Brumariu & Kerns 2013; Feldman, Bamberger, & Kanat-Maymon 2013; Kok et al. 2013; Lickenbrock et al. 2013; McElwain et al. 2008). Compared with children who do not feel secure, infants and toddlers who feel secure

> Express contentment and often joy when they are with you

> Mold on your body, draping on your shoulder or your tummy

> Feel less stressed

> Feel comfortable expressing many different emotions

> Are better able to manage intense feelings with your help

> Demonstrate more empathy for others who are looking sad or upset

> Experience a greater sense of self-worth

> Are more prosocial in play with peers—kind, loving, helping, and empathic

> Experience more turn-taking friendly interactions with adults and peers

> Expect fewer hostile responses from peers

> Are more cooperative and compliant with adults they know well

> Demonstrate fewer behavior meltdowns and defiance at age 3

> Are better able to problem solve and tackle challenging tasks

> Are more likely to tell an adult that they broke a rule (e.g., "I hit him") (older toddlers)

When the important adults in a child's life meet his needs for protection, affection, and emotional connections, they create a thriving relationship that affects how the child feels and thinks about himself and others and the way he learns. You are not spoiling children by meeting their needs. You are not pampering children or ruining them by showing them affection and admiration. You are not creating tyrants when you gently teach them what *to* do rather than what *not* to do. Rather, you are supporting children's inner strength, a desire to be with others, and emotional skills that will enable children to successfully meet challenges.

Relationships that meet infants' and toddlers' needs are supported through

> Mutually rewarding interactions between teachers and children and between peers

> Program practices that contribute to children's and teachers' well-being

Mutually Rewarding Interactions

Infant and toddler learning occurs within the context of mutually rewarding adult–child and child–child relationships that are equally satisfying to each partner. When an infant makes soft sounds and you respond with soft sounds while smiling and looking into the infant's eyes, you are engaging in a mutually rewarding interaction with the child. A toddler experiences a rewarding interaction with you when she shows you something she has discovered and you respond with enthusiasm.

Children are born primed to become capable learners. The ability of infants and toddlers to figure out patterns of behaviors, the goals of others, and how to solve problems is nothing short of amazing. They can only become capable learners, however, when their physical, emotional, and social needs are met through rewarding interactions and relationships with trusted adults (Cuevas et al. 2014; Mermelshtine & Barnes 2016). Those needs include the following:

> Secure protection and caring emotional connections

> Love and affection

> Adults who are mindful and sensitively attuned

> Empathy and compassion

> Contingent responsiveness

> Adults who value them as unique individuals

Following are ways to nurture relationships to meet these needs.

Provide Secure Protection and Caring Emotional Connections

When children feel safe and protected by the adults in their lives, they can use their energies to learn rather than for staying alert for danger or threats (Ebbeck, Warrier, & Goh 2018; Posada et al. 2013). You help an infant or toddler feel safe when you hold or comfort him when he is distressed. You help him feel safe when you respond to his communication cues, no matter how subtle, in kind ways, such as saying, "I want to keep you safe," as you take his hand to help him down from standing on a chair (Lieberman 2017). Staying with children for several years rather than moving them every year to a new room with new teachers also provides them with a sense of safety and trust.

You will know that an infant emotionally connects in a healthy way with you when she settles in to your body as you comfort her or when a toddler comes to you for emotional refueling (Biringen 2008; Mahler, Pine, & Bergman [1975] 2000). Emotional refueling occurs when infants and toddlers need your touch, smile, or holding to gain emotional energy for their next adventure slightly away from you. You provide emotional refueling when you are the one children return to when scared, tired, or in need of assurance and affection.

Pay close attention to children who do not appear to feel emotionally connected to you or other adults in your program. If infants and toddlers avoid or seem angry at you or are wary of you, you may feel frustrated, puzzled, or discouraged that the child is not responding to your

efforts. These children need your special attention. They do not yet feel safe with you. Their experiences with adults may have led them to expect that adults are inconsistent in their interactions with them—for example, warm and loving one minute and harsh with them the next (Kerns & Brumariu 2014; Pallini et al. 2019).

Work closely with the child's family and other staff to gain the infant's or toddler's trust. For example, always greet this child by kneeling down so that you are at her eye level and opening your arms to help the child feel protected, emotionally connected, and special. Consistency in your interactions and in the program schedule are critical.

Nurture Love and Affection

Love and affection are nutrients for a young child's soul, enabling them to become socially adept humans who care about others. Children love and give love when they *feel* loved.

> The first ingredient in attachment is love. The idea that paid caregivers "love" the children in their care may make some uncomfortable. Yet, no one would disagree with the idea that caregivers must have warm, nurturing feelings toward the babies in their care. Call it what you will; its essence is love. (Honig 2002, 25)

The term *affective mutuality* describes what happens when there is harmony between the adult and child. There is mutual affection. While teachers may not feel the same degree of love or affection for all children, each child needs to feel a teacher's warmth, tenderness, and positive regard.

Children who deeply trust that their favorite adults love them and think they are lovable trust themselves to try tasks even when they encounter great frustrations. Children who feel loved despite garbled speech, juice spills, toileting accidents, and loud wails when they are upset can devote their energies to growing into capable, hardworking, and joyous individuals. They can concentrate on relating well to others and learning language, how to navigate environments, how to manipulate toys and use materials to create, and how to feel comfortable with reasonable social rules (Honig 2014, 16).

Use Mindful and Sensitive Attunement Strategies

When you consider what a child is thinking and feeling in a particular situation, you are using *mind-mindedness* (Meins 2013). You are trying to read the mind and mood of the infant or toddler. For example, consider the following:

> What is an infant who grabs your hair thinking? Is he trying to hurt you? Most likely he is not. Could he find your beautiful hair glowing in the sunlight fascinating? Was his intent to *touch* your hair, but his hand *grasped* it instead?

> What is a toddler thinking who shoves another child? Is she feeling angry, or is her goal to express her desire to play with her peer?

Thinking about what is in the mind of the child requires a belief that children have goals. They are actively trying different strategies to accomplish those goals. Very young children generally are not intentionally hurting others. Rather, they have a desire to connect to others but often do not know how. They may hit or punch to try to relate to a peer. That behavior usually does not achieve the toddler's goal of playing with a peer, unless an understanding and empathic teacher understands the meaning of the child's hitting behavior and helps that child try another strategy that is more likely to be successful.

To understand what a child may be feeling or thinking, offer a comment. You might say, "It seems like you are feeling sad," or "You were trying to get Callie's attention, weren't you?" When you express what you think a child may be feeling or thinking, you may get it wrong. If so, the child will let you know! Keep trying to understand and verbalize what she is feeling or thinking. When infants and toddlers feel understood, they often smile, look satisfied, or continue relating and learning.

Teachers who use mind-mindedness offer comments that support children's language and cognitive development (Kirk et al. 2015). For example, when you tell a toddler, "You are smiling! You seem happy," she learns words to describe emotions. Using mind-mindedness comments also helps children learn to manage their behavior. If an infant appears to be gazing at a toy horse on a shelf and you say, "You really want the horse. I'll move it closer so you can reach it," you are both providing vocabulary and helping the infant understand how to think about his actions. Children who gain these tools show fewer behavior difficulties at 3 and 5 years of age (Meins et al. 2013).

It's helpful to talk with other teachers about what *they* think children are thinking. Take pictures and videos of the children, share them with families and team members, and talk with them about what they think the children are feeling and thinking. Together, you can get a more complete picture of each child.

Mind-mindedness involves *sensitive attunement*. Attuned teachers engage in nonverbal and verbal turn-taking "dances" with an infant or toddler. These dances require tuning in to children's body cues, sounds, or words and responding effectively. They require giving infants and toddlers time to take a turn in the interaction. The children feel acknowledged and like star communicators. This sensitive, attuned dance contributes to children's social and emotional functioning (Shai & Belsky 2017) as well as other areas of development.

Show Empathy and Compassion

Your consideration and helpfulness meet young children's biological need for warm emotional connections (Stern, Borelli, & Smiley 2015). By feeling empathy and then showing kindness, you demonstrate your positive regard for each child. These are necessary components of children's secure attachments.

A thorough understanding of child development allows you to more fully develop empathy for a child who is struggling. When you know about early motor development, you have kind feelings toward and patience for an infant who is trying hard to pick up a safe piece of food from the table. A teacher who understands toddler development is kind when a toddler who has difficulty sitting wiggles or likes to gallop around. A knowledgeable teacher shows compassion when an older toddler has a toileting accident, even when toilet learning started many months prior.

Think about how you show kindness to infants and toddlers. Do you feel and show compassion for an infant who cries often during the day or do you find yourself thinking of him as clingy or even a crybaby? Are you kind to toddlers who grab toys from other toddlers' hands because you know that toddlers are just learning how to ask others for toys? Do you thoughtfully reflect on why a toddler seems angry? Do you ask yourself, "How is the child feeling? How can I best help?"

Be Contingently Responsive

Contingent responsiveness means that you respond to each child's physical or verbal communication quickly and in a way that meets the needs indicated by the child's cue. For example, a toddler pulls on your leg. Does the toddler want you to follow him or does the toddler want you to pick him up to comfort him? You may try one strategy and the toddler quickly and emphatically lets you know that that is not what he wanted. You try another strategy and this time the toddler feels heard. The toddler does not need to yell, pinch, or bite to get attention. You are developing a strong emotional connection with the child. You are also teaching social skills by showing the child how humans try different strategies to get their own needs met and how they can meet others' needs.

In addition, you are giving each child the gift of *self-efficacy*—the belief that she is capable. When you clap your hands in response to an infant's clapping or delightedly eat the slice of pretend "cake" a toddler has offered you, you are helping children develop a sense of themselves as effective communicators, which contributes to their feelings of self-worth.

When you are contingently responsive, you model desirable social behaviors. Responding to children's frowns, cries, language, and needs offers the opportunity to show children how to comment, smile, make eye contact with others, and show kindness and interest in another person (Brophy-Herb et al. 2011). Most important, infants and toddlers learn that they are active agents who make things happen.

Value Each Child's Uniqueness

Each child has his own temperament style, interests, and strengths. When you focus on building relationships, you pay attention to each child's uniqueness.

Temperament

Temperament refers to a person's style of behavior. Since Thomas and Chess (1977) wrote about temperaments decades ago, there has been a great deal of research on temperament, including its influence on children's behavior and adults' responses to different temperament styles (Chen 2018; Grady & Callan 2019).

For example, some children will eat whatever food you give them, sleep easily, and do not protest much when another toddler takes their toys. Much of the time these infants and toddlers smile and seem contented. They are generally easy to soothe.

Some toddlers are intense and feisty. They eat intensely, play intensely and loudly, and show you how they feel—forcefully and passionately. These vigorous, lively, and spirited children typically have a high activity level.

Other children seem fearful. Children who feel shy or fearful may have a challenging time in child care and learning programs. They need your support to try new activities and engage with others. Take it slowly with these children. Try to read a story just with the child who feels fearful and perhaps one other child. If she seems hesitant to explore and play when outdoors, let her stay close to you until she feels comfortable. Create a cozy corner indoors with space for a few children to play together. If you support and encourage these children rather than push them, most become less inhibited as they grow older (Kagan & Snidman 2009; Rubin, Burgess, & Hastings 2002).

Other children may seem irritable at times, and it can be a struggle to meet their needs. Talk frequently with family members to understand what calms their children. Explore a variety of ways to comfort them. An infant, and possibly even some toddlers, may like you to wrap them tightly in a blanket in your arms. If they react to scratchy clothing, talk to families about removing tags from the children's clothing. You may need to feed them smaller amounts of food more frequently. These children may need your positive encouragement of their efforts to put a puzzle together, throw a ball into a basket, or build a tower with blocks. With sensitive, patient, and responsive interactions, these children usually become less irritable as they grow.

It's important to recognize that temperament is not destiny (Gensthaler et al. 2013; Stifter, Putnam, & Jahromi 2008). All children with different temperaments can successfully develop relationships and learn, and they are more likely to blossom when adults understand and appreciate their temperaments.

Interests and Strengths

Discover what interests each child and how she learns, then look for ways you can best support her. One infant loves to be on the move, turning over at a young age and then moving on to crawling and pulling up on any object in sight, including your leg. Another infant is content to sit for lengthy periods of time and pay close attention to something fascinating, like the way the sand from an egg timer drifts slowly down. A toddler who loves music may cherish cuddling up to you and singing along with you, but another toddler tells you "No sing" and puts her hand over your mouth. One older toddler might love rocks of many sizes and shapes and always have one in his pocket. Another child does not care about rocks, but if she sees a pile of sand, she is ready to leap into it. She loves to use her wet hands to mold sand into different shapes. As children's interests and skills develop and change over time, keep observing and providing a responsive environment for children to pursue their uniqueness.

Program Practices that Support Healthy Relationships

Primary care, continuity of care, appropriate group sizes, and developmentally appropriate teacher–child ratios are program practices that contribute to children's caring relationships with adults and peers.

Primary Care

Primary care is the recommended practice in early care and education programs. One teacher provides the primary care for a small group of children (Kovach & Da Ros-Voseles 2008). The teacher of this small group learns each child's cues for hunger, sleep, cuddly contact, and readiness for play. The teacher knows how to comfort the children, feeds and diapers the infants in her small group, and sits at a table with her toddlers at mealtimes. She interacts frequently with the children's parents to understand the children even better and involve families in their care and education. The children come to know and trust their primary caregiver. Because a teacher cannot always be with *just* the children in her primary care group, a second teacher knows each child well also.

Children typically develop a secure attachment to their primary caregiver and feel secure with the second teacher as well. When young children feel a secure attachment to one or two teachers in a program, they are more likely to relax, feel safe, have fun, and focus on learning (Ebbeck et al. 2015).

Continuity of Care

Continuity of care (COC) is a practice in which at least one teacher in a center-based program stays with a group of infants and toddlers for an extended period—typically two to three years. One way for a child to experience continuity of care is to be in a multiage group of children from birth to age 3 with the same teachers for three years. Another method, used more frequently, is for children to move to a new room with at least one of the same teachers. Teachers start with a group of infants and continue with them until they are 3, then loop back and start with a new group of infants (Choi, Horm, & Jeon 2018).

COC practice is based on attachment research. Children know their teachers and teachers know their children. Children with secure attachments to parents and teachers are less stressed throughout the day (Badanes, Dmitrieva, & Watamura 2012). Children do not have to adjust to new adults every year (sometimes more often). While COC is not widely used (Choi, Horm, & Jeon 2018), many early childhood education organizations recommend this practice (Lally, Torres, & Phelps 2010; NAEYC 2018; Sosinsky et al. 2016).

There are many benefits to COC, including the following:

> Teachers feel effective because they accurately and easily read children's nonverbal and emotional cues.

> Children are more likely to become securely attached to their teacher(s). Raikes (1993) found that 91 percent of infants who spent more than one year with the same teacher were securely attached.

> Teachers rate children in COC classrooms as having higher levels of self-control, initiative, and attachment (Horm et al. 2016).

> Toddlers experience higher levels of interactive involvement with their teachers and are rated by their teachers as having fewer problem behaviors compared with toddlers in non-continuity rooms (Ruprecht, Elicker, & Choi 2016).

> Children experience more meaningful relationships with peers (de Groot Kim 2010).

> Teachers and families build strong relationships. It is easier to share information that helps children thrive.

It might seem desirable for children to get used to being with different adults, but "a strong, relationship-based beginning with[in] the first three years buttresses children for the multiple transitions they will face in the future" (McMullen 2017, 49). Nevertheless, providing COC is challenging for administrators and teachers (Garrity, Longstreth, & Alwashmi 2016). Many teachers feel more comfortable with a certain age group. Moving with a group as children age requires learning how to nurture children through the vast changes in their social, emotional, physical, cognitive, and language development as they move from infancy to preschool. However, COC benefits children, teachers, and families greatly. Center program staff can move slowly toward the use of COC by engaging in many discussions concerning the benefits for children and the strategies to begin the practice.

Group Sizes and Teacher–Child Ratios

Group size and teacher–child ratio are two factors that relate to quality programs that support caring relationships and children's safety and learning. Total group size is important. Imagine an infant room with 12 infants. Even though there may be three teachers, the room will seem quite noisy and chaotic. Smaller group sizes benefit both children and teachers (de Schipper, Riksen-Walraven, & Sabine 2006; Sosinsky et al. 2016).

Teacher–child ratio best practices indicate how many teachers there are for a certain number of children. NAEYC (2018) recommends one teacher to four infants with a maximum class size of eight children and one teacher to six toddlers or twos with a maximum class size of twelve.

When you create a relationship-based program and engage in mutually rewarding interactions that meet children's needs, you become a part of their life story and journey. As they grow, they may have no concrete memory of you as their teacher, but the way you make them feel about themselves and others becomes a part of who they are. The child's body and mind will remember through long years and retain the knowledge of your gentle care.

This chapter supports the following NAEYC Early Learning Programs standards and topics

> **Standard 1: Relationships**
> 1.B Building Positive Relationships Between Teachers and Children

Chapter 2

Create Mutually Supportive Relationships with Families

Providing responsive care to infants and toddlers in centers and family child care homes requires close relationships between teachers and families. Families want to know that you understand and deeply care for their children, and their knowledge of their children is critical to your ability to provide a responsive program. Families should also know that you have great respect for them as children's first teachers. All interactions should be reciprocal—there is much for you to learn from families, and much they can learn from you.

Young children thrive when families and teachers work closely together. Working with infants and toddlers requires a *co-caring framework* for family–teacher relationships (Lang et al. 2016). A co-caring framework is a way of thinking about how you relate to the families of the children in your program that recognizes the importance of teachers and families working closely together for the benefit of everyone involved. While family members have the primary responsibility for their own child, teachers are often with infants and toddlers many hours throughout the day. This requires open communication and the joint creation of strategies for the way programs and families support children's development and handle routines such as feeding, toilet learning, and sleeping (Lang et al. 2016).

Create an Inclusive Environment for All Families

Each culture has its experiences, traditions, rhythms, values, habits, and beliefs. Each family has its own cultural practices and preferences and goals for children. Families should be able to see themselves and their cultures and communities represented and valued throughout the program in photographs, books, clothes and home items in the toddler dramatic play area, music, toys, written communications, and other materials. Create a welcome area (see more in Chapter 9) and greet everyone warmly when they arrive.

If you or your colleagues do not speak a family's home language, find other families or individuals from the community who may be able to assist, and learn some words in the home language to help families feel welcome. Provide written materials in families' home languages. Find out how each family would like to be involved in the program. Find other ways you can create an environment in which they feel welcome and appreciated.

Strategies for Communicating and Building Relationships with Families

It takes time to build trusting relationships with families. Reciprocal communication is critical from the very first time you meet a family and child. Following are ideas to build respectful and helpful relationships with families. Each strategy creates a stronger bridge to open, friendly, and beneficial communication.

> Create a program handbook for families that includes clear information about the philosophy, mission, curriculum, and policies of the program. Ask current and prospective families what additional information they would find helpful.

> Create a welcoming intake process that asks families about their goals for their children, sleeping and eating routines, their children's preferences and dislikes, guidance strategies used in the home, and cultural practices. Be sure to ask family members what they want and need from the program for their children.

> Invite the parent and child for a transition day(s). Before the child begins the program, invite the parent *and* the child to spend several hours in the program. Some children will need family members to spend additional days visiting

the program to feel comfortable in the new setting. This time allows you to learn more about a child's routines and preferences and gives family members an opportunity to model how to effectively interact with their child.

> Create a process for families and teachers to discuss questions and concerns. Parents often do not know to whom they should go with questions. Assign a "go-to" person(s) for each family (Banks 2018). Develop collaborative problem-solving strategies to use with families (see Chapter 13 for more detail).

> Create a daily communication strategy that provides for two-way information to be shared with families. Many programs exchange information by text, email, or portfolios using family communication software (Koralek, Nemeth, & Ramsey 2019). Learn what works best for your families and what kind of information they find useful to exchange. Let families know that you value their input.

> Get to know families. Beyond what you learn from their enrollment forms, find a little time whenever you see them to talk about activities they like to do as a family, their individual interests, who they consider an important part of their family, and knowledge and skills they might like to use in the program in some way.

> Create documentation panels (see Chapter 11) with families that focus on what children are doing and learning at home and in the program.

> Create newsletters and bulletin boards—ask families for ideas for topics. Include the schedule of the day and/or week; learning opportunities in each learning center; interesting websites, YouTube videos, and pamphlets; and information about community resources. Be careful not to overload families with information.

> Develop family potluck nights or informative events that families and children attend together.

> Encourage families to participate on advisory committees that have input on program policies and special events.

Challenges in Building Strong Relationships with Families

Both you and a child's family are invested in the child's well-being. When disagreements arise, it is helpful to keep this in mind. Conflicts may be rooted in cultural differences or practices that are different in the home and program. While a parent knows his child best, conflicts may arise when the teacher's knowledge of child development and guidelines for professional practice conflict with the parent's wishes. Total agreement may not always be possible, but understanding and respect can always grow (Isik-Ercan 2017). Sometimes a third party, such as a program director, may need to help brainstorm solutions that are acceptable to everyone involved.

When a parent expresses anger or concerns, use active listening. Fully hear and understand what she is saying and restate the message to be sure you have understood correctly, as the teacher does in this situation:

> Henry's mother is upset that the toddler is napping too long at the center and is not tired at night at bedtime. Katrina, Henry's teacher, says, "I understand that bedtime for Henry is challenging when he is not tired. That must be so frustrating when everyone else in the family is tired and Henry won't go to sleep. What would you like us to try?" The mother suggests that the staff wake him up after an hour. Katrina agrees to try that solution for a week. Each time, however, Henry is miserable after he is awoken. Katrina shares this with Henry's mother and says, "Is there another solution we could try? This one does not seem to work for Henry. Could we try an hour and a half?"

Sometimes you may be upset with something a family is doing. Perhaps you've noticed that when a parent has a day off he still brings the child to the program for the day. Remember that you do not know what life is like for that parent. He may need to cope with the challenges of parenthood with a day to rest, shop for food for the family, or exercise. He may be bringing the child because the child really wants to be in your program that day.

If a parent wants you to use physical punishment or other behaviors that your program believes harm children, listen to the parent's reasons so that you understand her thinking about the situation. However, firmly explain that the policies of your program do not allow you to use physical punishment. Refer to your program handbook for reasons the program does not allow teachers to use physical punishment with children (see Chapter 13). Explain the strategies you do use when children exhibit challenging behaviors and why. Keep the lines of communication open and encourage the parent to try a particular strategy that you have found to be effective.

Most families want teachers who genuinely like and enjoy their child, appreciate and support their child's strengths, and help their child develop and learn. Try to say something positive about each child each day to her family. Share what you see the child learning. Ask families to share what they see children feeling and learning at home. Listen to concerns and work collaboratively to find acceptable solutions for all. This is the essence of a co-caring framework, and it leads to strong, affirmative relationships between teachers and family members.

Support Family–Child Relationships

With infants and toddlers being separated from their families for some portion of the day, it's important to actively support family–child relationships. Here are a few ways to help ease separation and support family and child relationships:

> Encourage families to create a special goodbye routine with their children when they come to the program, whether it's reading a book together, finding a favorite play item, or waving from the window. Children will come to know what to expect and find the separation easier. Tell parents to *always* say goodbye rather than try to sneak out. This builds young children's trust that family members will return.

> If you do not speak a child's home language, ask families to help you learn some familiar words, phrases, and songs to help the child feel more comfortable.

> If a child has a challenging time separating from the parent, ask the parent to provide a safe bracelet, photo, or blanket that reminds the child that the parent still exists and loves them. Let the infant or toddler keep this reminder with him during the day.

> Create large, laminated photos of each child's family. Place the photos in a basket so that each child can retrieve and carry her family's photo around. Or create a small booklet for each child with several photos of the family. Mobile infants and toddlers can carry this book around with them all day if they wish, and some toddlers may even want to sleep with their books at naptime.

> Create a short communication form that goes home with the child each day. This includes what the child ate, diaper changes, a line or two about what the child did, and the child's likes and dislikes during the day. Some programs use a similar form that families can use to report briefly in the morning on a tablet attached to a table. Parents can report whether the infant or toddler had difficulty sleeping or did not eat breakfast or there was some other unusual event.

The quality of children's relationships with their families influences children's social and emotional development (van Berkel et al. 2015; Huang et al. 2017), behavior (Lorber & Egeland 2011), language development (DiCarlo, Onwujuba, & Baumgartner 2014), and cognitive abilities (Cuevas et al. 2014). When you build partnerships with families and seek to encourage children's bonds with their families, everyone benefits.

This chapter supports the following NAEYC Early Learning Programs standards and topics

Program Standard 1: Relationships
1.A Building Positive Relationships Between Teachers and Families
Program Standard 7: Families
7.A Knowing and Understanding the Program's Families
7.B Sharing Information Between Staff and Families
7.C Nurturing Families as Advocates for Their Children
Program Standard 8: Community Relationships
8.A Linking with the Community
8.B Accessing Community Resources

PART 2

How Infants and Toddlers Develop and Learn

- -

Part 2 describes the wonder of infants' and toddlers' development and learning. Each chapter discusses a developmental domain (emotional, social, language, cognitive, and motor) and strategies for enhancing development and learning in that domain. Let this section inspire you to participate in the exciting and fulfilling process of observing and supporting young children as they learn to "be" (Tayler 2015), becoming social, communicating, thinking and problem solving, and moving successfully.

Chapter 3

The Wonder of Learning to "Be": Emotional Development and the Self

Positive emotional development is an important key to young children's success in life. From their first days, infants have a strong need to connect emotionally to caring, responsive adults. Emotional development affects the quality of infants' and toddlers' lives now and in the future.

Emotional development includes children's

> Loving relationships with important adults

> Sense of self, self-worth, and self-confidence

> Identification and expression of emotions

> Gradual development, with adult help, of self-regulation and impulse control

Developing Attachments to Important Adults

Very young children form *attachments*—strong emotional connections—to adults who are important in their lives, including family members and teachers. Secure attachment relationships keep children safe from harm, support brain development by helping children manage both distressing and happy emotions, result in children with better attention spans, and help young children learn to communicate and develop mutually satisfying relationships with other adults and peers (Brock & Kochanska 2019; McElwain et al. 2014; Pallini et al. 2019; Vaughn et al. 2016).

Quality of Attachments

While attachment is critical to children's well-being, the quality varies from relationship to relationship. Attachments can be *secure, anxious/ambivalent, avoidant,* or *disorganized* (Ainsworth, Bell, & Stayton 1971; Honig 2002). When a child experiences a sense of safety and consistent responses to his needs with a particular adult over time, he is likely to form a secure attachment to that adult. When he does not, an insecure attachment (anxious/ambivalent or avoidant) or disorganized attachment may develop. Even if the attachment relationship between an adult and child is challenging, the child often behaves in a way to try to stay safe with that adult. That may mean that he avoids the adult so as not to make the adult angry or anxiously stays near the adult much of the time and explores the environment less than other young children (Moullin, Waldfogel, & Washbrook 2017).

> Mara (4 months) nestles into her teacher, who smiles at her often and holds her gently. Marco (7 months) looks at his teacher's face to determine whether a parent who just walked into the room and approached him is safe. He relaxes when he sees his teacher smiling at the stranger.

Mara and Marco are feeling secure with their primary teachers. If Marco's teacher smiles, he is more likely to accept a stranger or a new situation. Older infants and toddlers feel secure when you help them feel safe *and* loved *and* admired. This feeling of security allows them to explore a short distance away from you. When they are tired or scared or just need you, they dash back to you—their source of energy and their secure base or security blanket. With renewed energy and courage, they venture forth again to explore their ever-changing and exciting world.

Attachment provides children with a blueprint for other relationships; children learn how to relate to others based on their experiences over time with their attachment figures. Children who feel secure, compared with those who do not, are more kind, caring, and helpful, and they act in friendlier ways with teachers and peers. They also experience higher-quality friendships (McElwain et al. 2008).

Children may experience a type of insecure attachment referred to as an *anxious/ambivalent* (Ainsworth, Bell, & Stayton 1971; Bowlby 1980; Kok et al. 2013). The child learns to resist or cling to adults who behave in inconsistent ways with them or who frustrate them much of the time. While parents or teachers cannot always notice and respond to *all* of a child's attempts for help or attention immediately, it is when an adult's responses are *often* inconsistent that the child may learn unhealthy ways to gain attention. The child who persists at getting attention wants so badly to be with the adult, but when most of the adult's responses are unpredictable, the interactions are not satisfying to the child. She may become resistant, clingy, dependent, and possibly defiant toward the adult in continued attempts to get her emotional needs met.

Infants or toddlers even may seek negative attention from adults by "disobedient" behavior that will get them physical closeness such as an adult yelling at them. Be constantly aware of what children's attachment experiences may be, and realize that the child seeking attention *needs* your loving attention.

> Jana, an infant teacher, hears Sam (4 months) cry again from his crib after waking from his nap. Jana's co-teacher declares, "It's good for babies to cry. You know, it is good for their lungs." Jana responds, "If we let him cry, I think Sam will learn not to trust adults to be kind. Sam may also not trust himself to communicate his needs. He may begin to feel insecure with us."

To feel secure, Sam needs his teachers to be consistently responsive. He can then use them as a secure base from which he feels safe to explore his environment.

Ainsworth et al. (1971) referred to another type of insecure attachment as *avoidant* attachment. Think about how Nia is feeling in the following vignette.

> Nia's mother, Cara, is experiencing a great deal of stress. Cara was just laid off from her job. Nia (9 months) felt safe with her mother until her mother lost her job and became angry with everyone, including Nia. Cara does not have much support from her relatives. She feels as if Nia cries on purpose to wake her up at night, and she often yells at Nia to be quiet. Nia often sits quietly away from her mother in an apparent attempt to not make her angry.

The child who, like Nia, learns to avoid adults has already learned that one way to feel safe is to avoid a nonresponsive or an angry adult or one that does not like to touch or hold them. This comes at great cost to a child's sense of trust in adults. Sometimes young children who have learned to avoid adults may seem to look more mature and fuss less than other children do when they enter a program. They may play independently and act as if they do not care whether adults pay attention to them or not.

Infants and toddlers who experience chaotic, sometimes abusive, environments may experience a *disorganized attachment* and express rage. Infants as young as 6 months may hit and show rage when their care is wildly inconsistent or harsh (Hay et al. 2014). They may arch their backs when picked up, scratch others, and not let adults and peers come close to them. Unless they begin to experience consistently loving caregiving, they have difficulty engaging in healthy relationships (Belsky & Pasco Fearon 2002).

Child development research points to the need for a social "womb" that provides infants with the opportunity to (1) develop secure bonds with the people who care for them; (2) engage in protected and encouraged social, intellectual, and communicative exploration; and (3) build a positive self-identity and sense of others (Lally 2014).

Respond Promptly and Attentively

Your responsive interactions lead to secure attachments and predict young children's ability to initiate and take turns (Hedenbro & Rydelius 2014). You may hear an infant's soft cooing sounds. You then respond by looking into the infant's eyes and cooing back. You patiently wait for the infant to coo again. Through your responsive interactions, infants learn to take conversational turns and trust you to take care of them.

A toddler may show you his ball and how he rolls it. You may enthusiastically exclaim, "That is a blue ball. You rolled the ball right to me." You may make yourself available for a game of rolling the ball back and forth. The toddler learns how to take turns when playing. This skill of turn taking, learned during responsive interaction sequences with you, is associated with children's success with peers at age 4 (Hedenbro & Rydelius 2014).

Infant and toddlers become securely attached when their teachers

> Sensitively and kindly attune to the child's feelings and needs

> Respond promptly and appropriately to their distress

> Take interactive turns with children when talking to and playing with them

> Are consistently available emotionally and physically

The Quality of Attachment Can Change

The quality of children's attachment relationships can change to become more or less secure (Belsky & Pasco Fearon 2002; Booth-LaForce et al. 2014). If an infant or toddler feels insecure with a parent and the parent becomes more responsive, the infant may begin to feel secure. If an infant or toddler feels secure and the parent become less responsive, the infant may begin to feel insecure. The quality of a child's attachment depends on the quality of the adult–child interactions.

Provide an Emotional Buffer

As a teacher, you have a unique and important opportunity to help a child who does not feel secure experience a sensitive and caring relationship. You can be an emotional buffer for a child who has experienced an insecure attachment. Young children experiencing stress are more resilient if they have at least one person who cares for them generously and deeply (Sciaraffa, Zeanah, & Zeanah 2018). You can help children build *resilience*—capacity to recover quickly from challenging experiences.

> Tahani's early experiences with adults in her family taught her that adults are unpredictable. Now 11-month-old Tahani avoids these adults to feel safe. Because of her experience at home, she also avoids her teacher, Sheila, when she enters Sheila's early childhood program.
>
> Sheila understands that this infant needs to experience a caring adult who is consistently kind and responsive to her needs. The teacher warmly greets Tahani each morning, and she often sits by the child and talks softly with her. Sheila consistently smiles at her, and one day Tahani smiles back! When she is distressed, Sheila offers comforting words and gentle touches. Gradually, Tahani feels protected when she is with her teacher. She also learns that there are adults she can trust. And Tahani's family is able to help her feel protected again at home after the early childhood education center connects the family with resources in the community.

Attachment relationships are crucial for young children because they influence children's feelings about themselves and others, often throughout their lives. Each day children are learning whether an adult is trustworthy. The children are learning in some deep sense whether they themselves are truly worthy of love. And they are learning to love others. If infants and toddlers feel secure, they build resilience—the ability to persist at challenging tasks (such as building with blocks and building mutually enjoyable relationships) and adapt more easily to stressful situations.

Fortunately, and happily, young children can indeed become attached to several other adults beside their parents. Each of these attachments is a unique relationship between the child and that adult. In fact, a secure attachment with parents *and* teachers is a recipe for children's emotional, social, and learning success (Cassidy & Shaver 2016).

Gaining a Sense of Self, Self-Worth, and Self-Confidence

In their first three years, children are learning to "be" (Tayler 2015). They are learning who they are in relation to others. Are they lovable and worthy of love? Who loves them? Whom do *they* love? Are they competent? We want children to develop a healthy sense of self, self-worth, self-confidence, and self-motivation. A competent and comfortable sense of self drives their ability to learn and feel loved, and in turn, to be able to relate positively to others.

> Matthias's toddler teacher recognizes his strong need to be with her. When she changes another child's diaper, she often brings a stool Matthias can sit on to be beside her. While he's there, Matthias happily looks at a book and looks up often to smile at his teacher.

This teacher is contributing to Matthias's sense of whether he is lovable, competent, heard, and respected. This understanding and knowledge about himself will stay with him as he grows.

A sense of self develops slowly (Rochat 2003). Young infants are aware that someone helps them feel comfortable or not. They respond to gentle, respectful touch differently from rough, abrupt, or nonresponsive touch.

> Natalia (14 months) points to herself when someone asks her, "Where's Natalia?" and to her mother when someone asks, "Where's Mama?" When her favorite adults ask, "Who wants yogurt?" Natalia points to herself and says, "Me!"

Natalia is beginning to distinguish herself from others. Even older infants begin to recognize their name and will turn and smile when someone calls out it out. Toddlers learn to refer to themselves by their name, as when Kai says, "Kai want milk." By 2 years of age, children learn the word *mine* and use it frequently and with intensity.

Young children gain a sense of identity over the first three years that establishes whether they feel competent, worthy of love, and able to feel love for others. Your eyes often tell young children whether they are competent and loved. Your eyes can express admiration, delight, and understanding. They also can express anger, disapproval, and frustration. Always think about what kind of identity a child is developing through her interactions with you.

Learning How to Understand and Express Emotions in Healthy Ways

The growth of emotional development in infants and toddlers, including understanding and expressing feelings, is truly a wonder. A somber infant furrows her brow, a toddler is so sad that tears flow, and a 2-year-old angrily resists when you deny her a second treat. Over the first three years, children also begin capably to interpret and respond to others' emotions. They need your support as they progress on this journey.

Learning to Express Feelings

Young infants express their needs through crying, looking at something, making sounds, and body movements. They protest loudly when hungry or physically uncomfortable. They express distress, disgust, and interest. They love warm, engaging smiles and dazzle adults with their own contagious smiles by 2 to 4 months of age.

From 4 to 8 months, feelings of sadness, contentment, fear, and anger appear. Then surprise, delight, and happiness develop during the first year. Infants begin to recognize that others have emotions too. They often mirror the emotions of the people taking care of them.

One- to 2-year-old children may express embarrassment. "The child's self-conscious emotions such as embarrassment, pride, guilt, and shame demonstrate that the child is developing self-consciousness" (Ross, Martin, & Cunningham 2016). Have you seen a 2-year-old who hides behind your legs after other adults exclaim over an accomplishment of the child? A 2½-year-old may run to a corner of the room if he spills milk. He may be ashamed or fearful of a scolding. After a while in your care, he will learn that he can help clean the table after an accident. By reassuring him and showing him what he can do to help, you help him make amends rather than be ashamed.

Supporting Emotional Learning by Responding and Using Emotion Words

Research on how infants and familiar adults connect emotionally shows how vulnerable infants are to changes in another's emotional reaction. Split-screen research shows a mother (viewed on one side of a screen) interacting with her infant (viewed on the other side of a screen). When the infant's favorite adult has been engaging in cooing and smiling interactions and then turns away, the infant will try hard to get the adult's attention by making sounds or reaching out. If the infant's attempts are not successful at regaining the rapt attention of the adult, the infant will become worried and unhappy—and start drooling and crying (Tronick 2007). Infants develop expectations that caring adults will respond to them and when they do not, infants may fall apart emotionally. Your sensitive response is so important for children!

Infants and toddlers need adults who talk often about emotions with them. Begin with emotion words such as *sad, happy, surprised,* and *afraid.* Then progress to using words such as *frustrated, lonely,* and *disappointed.* Talking about emotions with very young children, even infants, helps children's emotional and social skills. When researchers taught mothers to talk about emotions with their toddlers, their children learned "simple words to express emotions, needs, and wishes, instead of acting out physically" (Brophy-Herb et al. 2015, 512).

In another study, teachers increased their talk about emotions with 2- and 3-year-olds. The children used more emotion words than another group who did not hear emotion words. These young children learned to use words to describe their own feelings and were more prosocial toward peers (Grazzani et al. 2016). You help children learn about emotions and demonstrate more caring behavior toward others if you use more emotion words with children, talk with them about their emotions, and help them understand others' emotions.

Perhaps not surprisingly, children who learn words for feelings are more likely to recognize feelings in others. Recognizing and describing feelings are powerful emotional and social tools.

Beginning to Learn How to Self-Regulate

An important job for caring adults is to help infants and toddlers learn how to *self-regulate*—to manage their own strong emotions and behaviors. During the first three years, young children learn how to express feelings rather than fall apart, calm themselves with the help of adults, and wait patiently (for a brief time) for food, drinks, diapering, and attention. This all takes time and consistent, gentle support from invested, sensitive adults. Self-regulation involves *co-regulation* with empathic adults in the early years (Gillespie 2015). Co-regulation occurs as adults support children's self-regulation. With your help, infants and toddlers learn a variety of strategies to calm themselves and express their feelings in healthy ways. For example, as you help a crying 5-month-old infant by cuddling her in your arms, she learns that she can trust adults to be there for her. This helps her learn how to regulate her strong feelings of distress.

When you provide a safe lap and embrace a sad toddler who needs an adult to help him express his worried feelings, the child is reassured that he is not alone and that adults will help him learn to manage strong emotions. Create a safe, cozy quiet area in the room for toddlers who can choose the area to regain calm by turning a book's pages or lying quietly and looking up to see stars on a sheet that floats above them. Young children who feel distressed take comfort with furry, washable stuffed animals to embrace. While you want young children to learn to self-regulate, co-regulation is needed throughout life. Even adults turn to trusted others for help when they are experiencing difficult emotions.

By helping infants and toddlers develop self-regulation skills, you contribute to their later health and social and academic success (Moffitt et al. 2011). If they enter kindergarten and often express anger through tantrums and hitting, for example, they will have challenges with both social *and* academic success. When you soothe infants' and toddlers' distress and help them learn words to express emotions, you are helping them build a solid tool kit of self-regulation skills.

Emotional Challenges: Stranger and Separation Anxiety

Jengo (8 months) screams when a stranger peeks into his stroller. Jengo is experiencing stranger anxiety.

— — —

Kiara's father gives her a kiss at the door of the family child care home and cheerfully says goodbye, but Kiara (11 months old) continues to cling tightly to her daddy's legs. Kiara's teacher realizes that Kiara is experiencing separation anxiety. The teacher crouches down so she is Kiara's height and can see the child's face. She says, "Hello, Kiara. Sometimes it is hard to say goodbye to Daddy. We are so glad to see you today. Would you please help me feed the gerbil? Here is his food. Thank you so much, Kiara." She takes Kiara's hand and walks slowly into the room. Kiara and the teacher turn around to wave goodbye to her daddy.

Two types of anxiety—stranger anxiety and separation anxiety—occur from approximately 8 months to 18 months of age. When a child has *stranger anxiety,* he shows distress when in the presence of someone unfamiliar to him. When a child experiences *separation anxiety,* he becomes anxious when separating from loved ones.

Comfort children who are feeling anxious, while recognizing that these two types of anxiety represent a new stage of development for children. Encourage parents of toddlers who are experiencing separation anxiety to create a special routine that is always used when saying goodbye. A routine might include the toddler showing the parent something special in the room. The parent then says, "Goodbye. I will see you after your nap." The parent and child hug, and off the parent goes. You are emotionally present for the child to be with as the parent disappears.

When older infants and toddlers experience stranger anxiety, introduce new people slowly. Encourage strangers to talk with you first so that the infant or toddler can see that you are not afraid. If a child sees you and the stranger smile at each other, she will feel safer in the stranger's presence. Explain to people that they should not expect to hold an infant or toddler without giving the child opportunities to see them often. Respect a child's own timetable for feeling comfortable with someone new.

As an infant or toddler teacher, you are a cherishing, nurturing person who helps each child feel confident, admired, and appreciated beyond measure. These foundations enable each child to feel treasured and to share love and affection with others.

This chapter supports the following NAEYC Early Learning Programs standards and topics

Program Standard 1: Relationships
1.F Promoting Self-Regulation

Program Standard 2: Curriculum
2.A Essential Characteristics
2.B Social and Emotional Development

Chapter 4

The Wonder of Belonging and Becoming Social with Peers

All children are social beings, and the process of becoming so starts early. Toddlers and even infants generally show great interest in each other and enjoy being with each other. Their still-developing social skills mean that there are conflicts, too, but with loving support from families and from understanding and knowledgeable teachers, young children gradually become competent social beings.

In the first three years, children are

> Developing a sense of belonging in a group

> Learning how to interact with peers and begin to develop friendships

> Learning how to be prosocial

Developing a Sense of Belonging

Infants and toddlers need to feel as if they belong in your group—that they are welcome, enjoyed, and admired. For all humans, the need to belong is a need second only to the need for food, safety, protection, and shelter (Maslow 1987). If young children feel part of safe, loving, cherishing communities, they are free to develop positive ways of relating to others and to be busy at the task of exploring the world.

Participating in programs that are responsive to their and other children's needs, toddlers gradually gain a sense of themselves as independent of others and understand the difference between "me" and "we" (McMullen et al. 2009). They begin to have the "other" in mind as well as their own needs and wants, although the latter is certainly more common in toddlers!

Children feel a sense of belonging when they experience an environment purposely designed for interactions and relationships. Place an infant on the floor with a peer nearby so that the two can touch (gently!), hear, and see each other. Toddlers love cozy areas with pillows for two or three children to gather. They hide in big open-face boxes that entice social play, excitedly chase bubbles, and gather for a short time with a teacher to sing a song about their names and other topics important to them. To support young children's sense of belonging, try to keep groups of children together as they grow older. This is called *continuity of group*.

Learning How to Be with Peers and Develop Friendships

Throughout the first three years, children progress from watching and playing alongside their peers to delightedly imitating each other as they jump from pillow stepping-stones to lining up train tracks together. They move from laughing with and showing toys to peers as young toddlers to pretending together at 3 years of age that one is a baby and the other is a parent. Arranging the environment to encourage interactions and supporting children's efforts to relate to others is important for early social development.

Enjoying and Being with Peers

Older infants and young toddlers may play beside each other, seemingly not paying any attention to the other child. Mildred Parten (1932) called this *parallel play*. But they are often quite aware of each other. When one child gets up and moves away, the other child may get up and leave, too. One child may drop a toy and the other toddler picks it up. They imitate each other and smile at each other (Wittmer & Clauson 2018).

The playful peer interaction of toddlers has been called the social "style" of toddlers (Løkken 2000). This style includes toddlers using their bodies to engage with each other. They follow and imitate each other, run and chase each other, and play peekaboo. Løkken noticed that the toddlers she observed were having conversations with their bodies—*kinesthetic conversations*—rather than with words. The toddlers she observed also enjoyed a "glee concert" as they laughed and had great fun with each other.

Observe this social style, the kinesthetic conversations, and the sparkling eyes in times of glee. If this social style is not happening, ask why it is not happening. Are toddlers too controlled in the program? Are they provided extended periods of time to play with each other in an interesting environment? Are teachers enjoying play with the children?

Developing Friendships with Peers

Relating to others and developing preferential relationships with some peers begins early. Children can begin to show friendship behaviors by age 1, engaging differently with some peers and seeking them out more often (Howes 1996). Toddlers more often respond to distress shown by their peers who are friends (Howes 1996) and may even grieve when a friend leaves their room or program.

Shin (2010) observed two toddlers across a semester at a child care center in New York City, focusing on the friendship that developed between them:

> **Emily (14 months) often greets Katie (13 months) with a hug and kisses. Emily comes to Katie, sitting on the floor, and sits down right in front of her. Emily says hi, Katie says hi back, and both girls laugh. Emily gives Katie a big hug and holds her tightly. She calls Katie's name repeatedly all afternoon.**

On the way back to the classroom from the park, Katie starts fussing. Emily points at Katie, sitting across from her in the group stroller, and gently touches her body. Emily reaches into her backpack and takes out a tissue. Emily tries to help Katie wipe her runny nose.

Reciprocity describes Katie's and Emily's interactions with each other. Even though these two girls are young, they find ways to comfort each other.

Friendly toddlers often return kind acts. Toddlers may expect that when one friend initiates a game, the other will respond. When one says hi, the other friend will say hi and possibly give a hug. There are mutual interactions and affection.

Give children time and space to create games that involve interacting in special ways with each other—imitating, chasing, giving toys to each other, and sitting beside each other. Keeping groups of children together (continuity of group) as they age and move into a different room is important to encourage friendships.

Becoming Prosocial

Getting along with others and acting in selfless ways are the work of a lifetime, but children begin to learn these and other social skills early. Prosocial feelings, such as kindness and empathy, and skills of helping, comforting, and taking turns develop during the first three years. Infants who receive tender care grow into toddlers and twos who begin to show tender care for others.

Developing Helping Behaviors

Older infants and young toddlers expect a teacher to help if a child is having difficulty with a task. In one study, children 9 to 18 months old saw a video character unable to reach its goal because of an obstacle in the way. Another character was able to reach the object. When a helper entered the picture, the children watching the scene looked longer at the character in need of help. The researchers concluded that the young children expected the helper to help the character in need (Köster et al. 2016). Infants and toddlers may be watching you and expecting you to help their peers who are crying or need help, and these are good opportunities to model helpfulness and care for others. They may well choose *you* as their model when they see you being kind and helpful to other children (Holvoet et al. 2016).

Even young infants prefer others who are prosocial (helping and giving) rather than antisocial (hindering and taking). For example, 5-month-olds watched scenes played out with puppets. One puppet (A) helped another puppet (B) open a box while a few minutes later another puppet (C) stopped (rather than helped) puppet (B) who was trying to close the box. When given an opportunity to choose puppet A or C, even these very young infants chose the helper puppet by reaching for it (Kiley Hamlin & Wynn 2011).

Toddlers often want to help others. In one study, 12- to 18-month-olds warned an adult by pointing to a dangerous, aversive object in her way (Knudsen & Liszkowski 2013). Toddlers may give toys to children who are crying or run to you for help when a peer feels distressed. They model the words of comfort they have witnessed from you and may gently pat a distressed toddler on the back.

> Two toddlers, Manuel and Caleb, are outside playing. Caleb rides his tricycle on a sidewalk around the edge of the playground. Manuel notices that a cardboard box is directly in Caleb's path. Manuel runs quickly to remove the box before Caleb rounds the corner on his tricycle.

Give toddlers opportunities to help each other. For example, if a toddler needs help carrying two milk crates on the playground, encourage the child to ask another for help.

Toddlers are more likely to help other toddlers for whom they feel sympathy (Hepach, Vaish, & Tomasello 2013). To develop sympathy and encourage helping behavior, say to a peer, "Look, Mei is crying. She is sad. What can we do to help her feel better?"

Here are some additional ways to teach young children how to help others:

> Point out when another child is struggling with a task or feels distressed to encourage toddlers to take the perspective of that child and offer help.

> Call attention to others' emotional expressions (for example, looking upset) so children learn when another person needs help.

> Problem solve with a child, looking for simple ways to help another child.

> Continually model helping behaviors and talk about why and how you are helping a co-teacher or child.

Developing Empathy

Empathy includes understanding the thoughts and feelings of others and responding with care and concern (Bloom 2017). Infants may possibly cry when another infant cries. This contagion may feel like chaos in a center's infant room. Sometimes an infant sucks his own thumb rather than cry when hearing another child's distress. Think of these behaviors as the beginnings of infants developing empathy and becoming prosocial. As a teacher comforts Rashid, she could say to Teisha in a warm tone, "You heard Rashid cry. It is hard to hear someone cry, isn't it? I will help him calm down and feel better."

Older infants and young toddlers show concern for others (Roth-Hanania, Davidov, & Zahn-Waxler 2011). Here is one example of the many kind behaviors between older infants and young toddlers observed by McMullen and colleagues (2009):

> We were playing in the large-motor room, and Rosie [a young toddler] needed her nose wiped. We noticed this because Matilda [a young toddler] walked over to the box of tissues and took one out, walked over to Rosie, and rubbed her face with the tissue, making a smeary mess all over her face! (24)

Appreciate children's efforts to help each other. In this case, the teacher might say, "Thank you, Matilda. You noticed Rosie's runny nose. You really wanted to help Rosie feel better."

Many 2- and 3-year-old children become alarmed when they accidently hurt a peer. If they help repair the harm, they become less distressed (Hepach, Vaish, & Tomasello 2017). When possible, include toddlers and twos as helpers when trying to comfort a distressed child.

Learning How to Share and Take Turns

Toddlers might share a small space on the floor next to you as they listen to a story. Sharing their materials, toys, and food, however, is more difficult. Toddlers are learning the difference between the concepts of *ownership*, *possession*, *mine*, *yours*, *taking turns*, and *sharing*. Problems or puzzlements these young children are trying to understand include the following:

> When does one own a toy or just possess it temporarily, like a tricycle?

> How long is a toy mine?

> If I put a toy down to go look out the window, isn't the toy still mine when I come back?

> If I give toys to someone else but then want them back, shouldn't that person give them back to me?

> How can I be sure no one will touch my block structure if I leave it to go get a snack?

Young children learn turn taking before sharing, which is dividing resources. Sharing is when one person has two cars and gives one to a friend. Taking turns occurs when one person has a toy, plays with it, and then gives it to someone else so that person has a turn to play with the toy. Encourage children to take turns with toys or spaces. However, you also want to encourage persistence and focus. If an infant is focusing on examining a toy, do not expect her to take turns until she finishes playing with it. If a toddler is deep in play with a truck or doll, the toddler is using that toy. He should not be expected to take turns or share the toy during this play episode. Encourage the child who wants a turn to find another truck or doll and perhaps play next to the other child; in this way you encourage peer social relationships.

One way to prevent conflicts is to provide multiples of the same or similar toys in the environment so children can have their own. This does not solve every problem, and you will sometimes need to make delicate decisions about sharing in the moment. When there are conflicts over a toy, you might offer a comparable toy for the second toddler to examine or use.

> Martin intensely wants the big doll in the hands of another child. Even though Martin has a doll too, the doll in Kareem's hands looks much more attractive as Kareem is moving the doll around. The teacher notices the intent look on Martin's face and his movement toward Kareem. She crouches down so Martin can see her face and says quietly, "Kareem is playing with the doll. He is feeding it. Would you like a bottle to feed your baby? I see one over here. Let's go get that other bottle."

Toddlers' ability to share is developing. After observing 18- to 24-month-olds, Ulber, Hamann, & Tomasello concluded that "young children are not selfish, but instead rather generous, with resources when they are dividing them among themselves" (2015, 228). The researchers gave pairs of toddlers a box with four toys. The toddlers shared the toys equally 44 percent of the time, unequally 37 percent of the time, and not at all 19 percent of the time.

Facilitating Prosocial Development

Teachers need to be *prosocial detectors* who appreciate, notice, and encourage infants and toddlers who are helping, defending, comforting, or using other behaviors that benefit another person. Comment on these behaviors and their effects: "Thank you. You helped Wyatt. He looks so happy now." You can change the ambiance of a room from negative to positive when you expect, observe, and support prosocial behavior.

Help children understand the feelings of others, and verbalize your own empathy with infants' and toddlers' struggles in order to help children feel understood. Saying "I can tell you are feeling sad that we cannot go outside today. It is raining so hard. You wish the rain would stop so we could go outside" helps infants and toddlers feel soothed *and* learn how to empathize with others.

Modeling prosocial behavior is one of the most important things that you can do to help young children become prosocial. Infants and toddlers are stellar imitators. *The way you are influences the way that they will become.* In one study, 16-month-old toddlers who watched adults help or not help another person then were given an opportunity to help (Schuhmacher, Köster, & Kärtner 2018). Those who observed the helping adult were much more likely to help when given a chance. Consistently model kind, helping, caring behaviors for young children to imitate, and you will create a culture of caring in your program (Quann & Wien 2006; Wittmer & Clauson 2018).

Helping Children Negotiate Conflicts

Conflicts are common among older infants and toddlers. Often, conflicts begin when children are exploring. A toy in the hand of another toddler looks much more attractive than that same toy sitting on the floor. A toddler may grab the attractive toy right out of the hands of the other toddler. Conflicts also occur when one child feels that another child is intruding into her space.

This age group definitely needs your help to turn conflicts into learning opportunities (Wittmer & Clauson 2018). Infants and toddlers are just learning how to control their behavior, use language to express their needs, and problem solve. Your goal is to help young children learn cooperation and negotiation skills to prevent conflicts and to resolve conflicts. Always think about how the relationship between two children who engage in a conflict can be restored to become harmonious.

Following are some strategies for resolving conflicts with toddlers and helping them learn emotional and social skills so that they can create and sustain enjoyable relationships with peers. Endeavor to engage in problem solving *with* toddlers, not *for* toddlers (Gloeckler & Cassell 2012).

> Move in closer to the children to observe how they handle the conflict. It is tempting to move quickly to intervene in an effort to avoid a child getting hurt or extremely upset, but waiting a bit gives toddlers an opportunity to resolve their own conflicts.

> Comfort and comment on the feelings of each child: "You seem to feel worried." Or, "I can see that you feel angry." You are helping children learn the words to express their feelings *and* take the perspective of the other child.

> Give children the words (or sign language) to express their feelings. Over time, they will begin to use the words on their own.

> Ask the toddlers to tell you what they want. Many toddlers will not be able to do this at first. If toddlers cannot explain, state the problem as best you can. Comment on each child's goal, offering your best guess. "Dashante, you want to play with this ball. Nathaniel, you really want this ball, too. Both of you want to play with this ball."

> Ask, "What can you do to solve this problem?" Many toddlers will not be able to think of solutions at first. If they can't offer solutions that build strong relationships, give them some choices:

  * You roll the ball back and forth to each other.

  * You take turns trying to throw the ball in this basket.

  * You each hold the ball for one minute. I will count for you.

  * We find another ball so that *each* of you can have a ball to play with.

> Ask what they would both like to do. Although many options are listed in the example above, usually only give toddlers two choices, and model these choices for the children.

> If a toddler is concentrating on a task and another child interrupts, then help the child who disrupted the play to stand back, observe, and then ask if he can play, too. If the concentrating toddler says no, help the second child wait until the first is finished. Remember that you do want to support toddlers' ability to focus on finishing a task.

Social Challenges: Peer Rejection, Withdrawal, and Aggression

Toddlers who frequently act in aggressive ways are more likely to be ignored or rejected by their peers. Other toddlers may withdraw from contact when they feel fearful or unsure of their abilities. These children need your help. They are more likely than their friendlier peers to continue experiencing social challenges as they grow older. Observe the children, document what you see, come up with some options to try, and work with the children's families to create a plan to help these children. For example, you might keep a child who withdraws from other children or is rejected by them by your side for a while to help her enter group play. Take many responsive conversational turns with the child so she learns how to take turns. Show affection to her. Help her feel safe and secure so that she will begin to feel comfortable venturing forth with others. Give the child favorite materials such as bubbles to share with peers.

> Ava, a toddler, picks up a toy hammer used to play music on a xylophone. As Ava walks around the room tapping on furniture and then the window, the other toddlers move quickly out of her way. At other times Ava often hits them, and they often avoid Ava and do not join her in play. Ava's teacher, Valeria, decides to help the children in the room view Ava as a helper, not a person who hurts others. With the support of other teachers and Ava's family, Valeria develops some steps for all of the adults to address the behavior they are seeing:
>
> ❭ Everyone observes Ava in a variety of settings and discusses the observations. From this, the adults notice that Ava hits when she seems to feel crowded by the other children.
>
> ❭ All adults try to be more responsive to Ava to help her trust adults and learn interactive turn-taking skills. They discover what soothes Ava when she is upset, such as patting her back gently, and use that technique to help Ava become calm and express her needs.
>
> ❭ A teacher stays close to Ava to help her use words to express her feelings rather than hit. This sometimes means giving Ava words to try to use.
>
> ❭ Teachers notice Ava's prosocial behav times wiors and give her many opportunities to help other children, such as taking a tissue to a crying child or being a snack helper. Teachers comment on Ava's specific prosocial behaviors so that other children can begin to see Ava as a helper.

All infants and toddlers need your help to create an environment and opportunities that support positive peer social development. Children who experience rejection or avoidance from other children or who withdraw need your special guidance during these critically important years (Fox et al. 2013; Kiel, Premo, & Buss 2016).

This chapter supports the following NAEYC Early Learning Programs standards and topics

Program Standard 1: Relationships
1.C Helping Children Make Friends

Program Standard 2: Curriculum
2.A Essential Characteristics
2.B Social and Emotional Development

Chapter 5

The Wonder of Learning to Communicate

The ability to communicate nonverbally and with words is one of the most powerful ways that children learn to be and belong. Using body movements, facial expressions, gestures, words, sign language, and/or spoken words to communicate helps children make their needs and wants known and gives them joy and great satisfaction. Also, when children listen to and decode the feelings of others, they begin to understand the needs of others—a crucial social skill. The ability to communicate enables young children to create affectionate connections with each other and express their unique personalities. Infants and toddlers are developing both their receptive (comprehension) and expressive (what they are able to communicate) language abilities.

Developing Receptive Language Skills

Young children understand so much more than they can say. Infants come into this world ready to learn any of the languages that they hear. They can distinguish the difference in all sounds (phonemes) spoken throughout the world. By 6 months, however, they tune in to the language(s) that they hear every day and mimic those sounds (Kuhl 2007). During their first year, as adults talk and sing with them, children learn the patterns of language, such as which sounds and words are likely to follow others (Hay et al. 2011). For example, as children hear lots of language, they come to expect that an object rather than an action will follow the word *the*. Infants and toddlers process these rules or patterns of their home languages as they hear and engage in language interactions with their favorite adults.

At 1 year, children still understand much more than they can say. In one study, 12-month-old infants watched two researchers. Each adult played with her own ball and then hid it. If a researcher said to the infant, "Get my ball," the infant retrieved the specific ball that the researcher had been playing with. If the researcher said to the infant, "Get the ball," the infant retrieved either of the two balls. These young children understood that when the adult used the possessive word *my*, she wanted the specific ball that she had been playing with (Saylor, Ganea, & Vázquez 2011). These infants had learned the unique differences between the words *the* and *my* by 1 year of age.

A young toddler may make a beeline for her chair at a table when you ask, "Who is hungry?" As children grow older, they understand more complex directions. For example, they may understand, "Please, get your shoes *and* your coat. We are going outside." Observe older infants' and toddlers' receptive language carefully because children typically understand much more than they say. If a toddler cannot follow a sequence of two directions, talk with the family to suggest that a specialist check the child's hearing.

Learning Vocabulary and the Meaning of Words

In the first three years, children learn to understand and express a large number of words (*vocabulary*). They are also learning the meaning of many words (*semantics*). The number of words that children learn to understand and use is important. Children who have larger vocabularies at 24 months are more likely to learn better and demonstrate better behavioral control in kindergarten (Morgan et al. 2015).

Children learn more words when

〉 Adults respond to their gestures, sounds, and words with language

〉 They have opportunities to make sounds and talk with adults who listen

〉 They hear many words in context as they are eating or playing

For example, use the word *stomping* as you all stomp out to the playground or children stomp in mud in their boots!

Infants and young toddlers learn words more easily when you

> Gesture to direct the child's attention as you say words (de Villiers Rader & Zukow-Goldring 2012), such as pointing to a person or object and then saying the name

> Look where a child is looking and then name the object or person

> Are a "generous word giver" (Honig 2001, 31), describing the child's actions and feelings

> Expand children's language by adding a word or two (e.g., the toddler says, "Bird," and you add to the sequence and meaning when you respond, "The bird is flying")

> Use self-talk—talking about what you are doing as you are doing it

> Use parallel talk—talking about what the child is doing

All these strategies create opportunities for joint attention—that shared time when you and the child tune in to each other.

The Importance of Joint Attention

Padma (just 1 year) points with her index finger at the puppy that walks by the fence around the outdoor play area. Padma points and then looks up at her teacher to see if he is looking at the puppy. The teacher looks where Padma is pointing and exclaims, "Oh, a puppy!" The teacher and Padma share a wonderful moment of joint attention.

One-year-olds point to get adults to look at an object of interest. Sometimes, with an inquisitive glance toward you, they expect you to name the object, person, or animal. This joint attention is important. It is a signal of interconnectedness and gives you the opportunity to use descriptive words with a child and share moments of delight. Joint attention benefits older children, also. If a toddler runs to a window to see a rumbling truck go by, join her by the window. Your joint attention supports the child's focused attention and language development. Reflect on your time with children and ask yourself, "How many joint attention experiences have we had today?"

Learning Expressive Language Skills

One of the most important aspects of teaching children birth to 3 is helping them learn the names of objects, people, and actions; say or sign those words; and put words together to communicate more complex ideas. Before infants learn words, however, they cry, coo with throaty sounds, babble, and communicate with gestures.

Infants cry to express their distress. Younger infants coo (soft vowel sounds) and older infants babble (*ma, ba, da*). Later, they babble by stringing syllables together (*ma-ma, da-da, ba-ba*). Young toddlers begin to use words to communicate. Usually, a first word appears by 1 year of age, but some children use several words by their first birthday.

Toddlers will often jabber: they sound as if they are asking a question or telling you something super important, but it is impossible to understand what they are saying. They are putting many sounds together, often with great stress on certain sounds. They may even place their hands on

their hips and jabber as if they are telling you the most critical information in the world. If it seems as if they are asking for something by their questioning intonation, you might say, "Show me what you want." Many toddlers are satisfied if you nod your head and say something like, "That's quite a story. Thank you for telling me." You support children's desire to communicate when you are responsive to their attempts to communicate, even if you don't fully understand what they are saying.

As you hear young toddlers say more and more words, they often beam when you enthusiastically respond to these words. Responding to a child's communication bid helps him feel like an effective communicator. When a 1-year-old says, "Doggie," build on what he says by responding with something like "Yes, a nice dog" or "Brown dog" or "The dog is running." Your responses encourage children to continue communicating and learn new vocabulary.

By 18 months, toddlers begin to put several words together and invent creative sentences. Soon they are saying two-word sentences such as "Bye, papa," "Me seeping [sleeping]," and "Me running." Two-year-old children may put several words together, like "Put it right here."

You will notice how toddlers and twos are learning how to sequence words (syntax) to make sense. They learn that instead of saying "Eat kitty," they say the noun (kitty) before the action (eat), as in "Kitty eat." Toddlers also add beginnings and endings to words (morphemes). First you will hear them add the morpheme -*ing* to words, as in the phrase "Me jumping." Then they add the morpheme -*s* as in the words *balls* and *cows*. Then they add an -*ed*, as in "I jumped." It's exciting to hear a child begin to add endings to words. Share your excitement with her family so that everyone celebrates the child's remarkable growth in language development.

When children say something like "I runned," they are attempting to apply what they have learned about the rules of language (Brown 1973). Two-year-olds learn to use words such as *played*, *jumped*, *cried*, and *hopped* when talking about what happened in the past, and many think that they should now add *-ed* to *all* action words when they want to talk about the past. They may say "sanged," "ranned," and "sawed." As these are words children don't hear spoken, clearly they aren't just parroting what they hear; they are figuring out the rules of language by listening and engaging in conversations with attentive adults in a language-rich environment.

Soon, as you model for the children, they will learn to use the exceptions to the rule as in the words *sang*, *ran*, and *saw*. If they say "sanged," model the correct usage by saying, "Yes, you *sang* a song." Directly correcting a child by saying "No, we say 'sang,' not 'sanged'" may cause the child to stop communicating with you as much. Children will learn the correct forms as you model and engage in meaningful conversations with them.

Each child develops "a unique, expressive voice" (Mayor & Plunkett 2014). You never know what a child will say. A 1-year-old may surprise us by saying "bite" when he sees us eating food and wants a bite. Or an almost 3-year-old may ask, "Why I kick the wall?" Listening to each child's unique expressive voice helps you know each child better and immensely enjoy her budding language efforts.

Learning Pragmatics

Infants and toddlers are also learning the pragmatics of language, or how to use language in different social situations. Older infants and toddlers learn that they can use words to describe, demand, ask, request, state a fact, and express what they are feeling, like love, worry, and displeasure. They feel like powerful communicators when they use words for different purposes, especially when you respond.

Controlling the loudness of their voices is challenging for young children. Some settings require quiet, such as when other children are napping. It is difficult for toddlers to learn not to yell in such circumstances—after all, they yell as loudly as possible on the playground! They are just beginning to learn *how* to use voice tones and adjust language in different social situations. Learning to whisper is a challenging task. Patiently model how to use language in different settings. Young children will gradually learn how their families and cultures use language to match different situations.

Learning Prosody, or the Music of Language

> Ayo, a 1 year old, says, "Cup?" pointing to his cup. His teacher says, "Yes, cup. It is a red cup," also pointing at the cup. Several months later, Ayo says, "Cup?" in a questioning voice. His teacher replies, "Yes, there's the cup," pointing to a cup out of Ayo's reach. Then with an insistent tone, Ayo demands, "Cup." His teacher says, "Oh, you want the cup. Here it is," and hands him the cup.

Listen to, interpret, and appreciate the emotions expressed by infants' and toddlers' different tones. An infant's cry may express pain, hunger, or a need for attention. Toddlers express many emotions—being happy, sad, frustrated, demanding, or fearful. When you respond by validating

a child's expressed emotions ("You sound hungry!" or "You are so excited to see the caterpillar again!"), you help children regulate their emotions. Your sensitive attunement also creates moments of emotional connection and helps build satisfying relationships with young children.

Young children respond to your voice tones as well. By 5 months old, infants smile in response to approving voice tones and become distressed in response to disapproving tones (Fernald 1993). For infants and toddlers, both *what* you say and *how* you say it are important.

Learning Two or More Languages

Infants and toddlers may be learning two or more languages at the same time, including sign language. When they do so, their thinking skills are enhanced. Infants and toddlers who learn two or more languages are better able to remember and also to regulate their behavior than children learning only one language (Crivello et al. 2016). Children who are learning two languages must often choose between two words (e.g., *ball* or *pelota*) depending upon the situation. This requires focus and flexible thinking. The bilingual brain becomes nimbler and more efficient than the brain of someone learning one language (Kluger 2013).

Learning two languages at the same time does not harm infants' and toddlers' language development. Young children who are learning two languages simultaneously often understand much more than they say. They may use fewer words in each language than children learning one language. However, the total number of words expressed is the same (Poulin-Dubois et al. 2013). The number of words in each language depends on the amount of time a child hears each one. More exposure equals more language (Poulin-Dubois et al. 2013).

Support infants' and toddlers' learning one or two or more languages by

> Encouraging families to speak to their children in their home language (if that is their desire)

> Engaging in face-to-face, social interactions with children; research shows that infants and toddlers do not learn sounds and words of another language by watching or listening to recordings of that language (Kuhl, Tsao, & Liu 2003)

> Learning and using meaningful words in a child's home language in the program

> Encouraging volunteers to read books and engage in conversations in the home language with a child who is being exposed to a new language in the program

Learning Sign Language

Many parents and teachers teach hearing infants *and* infants and children with hearing challenges to use sign language. Those adults who teach signs to their infants who hear well often believe that learning signs enhances verbal language development. However, a study of infants and toddlers from 9 through 18 months of age found that learning sign language did not *help or hinder* language development in the children without hearing challenges (Seal & Depaolis 2014).

There are other benefits of children learning sign language. Researchers who followed 40 infants from age 8 to 20 months found that mothers of the children learning sign language were more responsive to their infants' nonverbal cues. When an 11-month-old signs "eat" before he can say the word, adults are often surprised that the child is thinking about food and can ask for it. An advantage of children learning sign language, then, may be that adults experience mind-mindedness (Kirk et al. 2013), knowing and respecting that infants are thinking. This encourages a deeper emotional connection between the child and adult and more intentional, sophisticated language from the adult.

In addition, infants and toddlers who learn some sign language may experience less frustration when they are trying to communicate their hunger, thirst, or tiredness and don't yet have the words they need. They feel like powerful communicators early in life.

Facilitating Children's Language Development

Pointing to and showing objects as you name them helps young children focus on the object of interest. You want both you and the child to experience joint attention—attending to the same thing at the same time. Joint attention includes *observing* what children are doing, *labeling* their actions, and *naming* the objects of their focus. These are other strategies that help infants and toddlers learn new words:

> Using *parentese*, or child-directed talk

> Being responsive

> Asking meaningful questions

> Talking during routines

> Reading stories and singing songs

Parentese

Parentese, or child-directed speech, describes several elements of language and tone that many adults use with infants and toddlers. When adults use parentese, they repeat words, speak in a higher tone of voice, use shorter sentences, and use diminutives, such as *piggie* instead of *pig*. They exaggerate the sounds in words and use different tones of voice when saying the words. Saying words with emotion and changing the pitch of your voice help infants and toddlers tune in to language. Adults worldwide use child-directed speech when talking to infants (Ramírez-Esparza, García-Sierra, & Kuhl 2014).

Child-directed speech is more effective when adults engage with infants and toddlers one-on-one. Imagine the following scenario:

> An infant focuses intently on his teacher's face and mouth as she gently strokes the infant's toes and says in an exaggerated, singsong voice, "I see your toes. Your toes are soooo little!"

Notice that the adult uses the word *toes* repeatedly, and the infant feels his toes touched as the adult says the word. Child-directed speech also includes waiting for the infant to respond with sounds. A relationship of trust develops and grows with this type of sensitive interaction that helps increase children's vocabulary.

Responsive Serve and Return

> Felipe toddles to his teacher, Carina, and declares, "Nana." Carina, who is sitting on the floor, smiles and replies, "Hi, Felipe. Nana, banana." Felipe smiles and says, "Bana."

Adult responsiveness is the key to unlocking the potential of language learning. When you engage in a language-building technique called *serve and return* (Center on the Developing Child, n.d. b), the turns you take with an infant or toddler are similar to what occurs in a tennis match. The child *serves* with a sound or word, and you return the serve with sounds, descriptive words, or a hug. Or *you* serve sounds and words and then wait attentively for the child to respond. This language-learning strategy is enjoyable for both children and adults, helping to build a strong relationship, and it supports language learning by helping children understand how conversations work.

Responsiveness works well for helping young children from birth to 3 learn vocabulary and how to communicate. When you engage in a babbling conversation with infants, infants babble more and use new sounds (Goldstein & Schwade 2008). An infant says, "Ba," and the responsive adult looks into her eyes and tenderly says, "Ba, da." After hearing these sounds in responsive ways over days and months, the infant may repeat, "Ba, da." She has learned a new sound because of your warm responsiveness.

When adults respond, children *learn that they can communicate*. They learn that "language is a tool that enables intentions to be socially shared" (Tamis-LeMonda, Kuchirko, & Song 2014, 121). Learning that they are effective communicators is one of the most important lessons young children gain from you.

Using Questions to Increase Children's Language

For infants and toddlers to increase their language skills, you must give them time to talk as they play and engage in daily routines. Children also talk to you if you are careful and sensible in the questions you ask them. After observing one hundred 2- and 3-year-old children in child care programs, Wittmer and Honig (1991) found that the children answered choice questions 100 percent of the time; however, teachers asked very few of these types of questions. Toddlers and twos love true choices. When you ask older infants or toddlers if they want juice or milk, for example, you are building their autonomy and their language development.

Talking Through Routines

Routines are wonderful opportunities for engaging children with language and encouraging them to communicate. Take advantage of diapering and feeding to engage one-on-one with a child. For example, when you're diapering a child, comment enthusiastically when he holds up his hand: "That's your hand, LeBron! Where are your legs? Oh, there they are," as if you are surprised to find them. The infant may smile and kick his legs.

Ask yourself the following questions about how you support language development during routines and play.

> Do you talk with children as you diaper them and feed them, giving them many opportunities to express themselves?

> Do you sit with toddlers and twos to support language development when they are eating snack and lunch?

> Do you engage in serve and return conversations with all children, no matter where they are in their language learning, during routines and play?

> Do you narrate children's play? For example, you might say in an exaggerated tone to Amelia, who is trying to stack one block on another, "You are putting a *small* block on top of the *big* block."

> Do you ask open-ended questions rather than closed questions that have just one answer? Open-ended questions let children explore: "How is the bear feeling?" There is not one correct answer to open-ended questions. Closed questions allow for yes or no or one correct answer: "What is this color?"

> Do you ask thoughtful questions that give children an actual choice? For example, you might ask a toddler, "Do you want to walk back to the door with me or run?" Questions that truly offer toddlers a choice build their sense of autonomy and language development.

> Do you listen carefully to the sounds, words, and sentences that children say during routines and expand their language when it is your turn to talk by adding a sound, word, or sentence?

Reading Stories and Singing Songs

Books spark young children's interests and language learning as adults show them pictures, name the animals and objects, and listen as children excitedly respond. Books are a mortar that cements relationships when you warmly hold infants and encourage toddlers and twos to snuggle near you when you read. Because reading and singing to and with children is so important, we will discuss this topic much more in Chapter 12.

Language and Communication Challenges

Children with language delays and children with autism spectrum disorder will require teachers to be responsive to their needs. Remember that each child is an individual with unique strengths, personalities, and needs.

Language Delays

Parents and teachers often have difficulty knowing when a child is experiencing language delays. In one study, researchers considered boys who spoke fewer than 10 words and girls who spoke fewer than 17 words at 24 months to be late talkers. Late talkers at 2 years were at risk for later language and school readiness challenges at age 5 (Hammer et al. 2017). Children who are late talkers, unless they are learning two or three languages, will benefit from hearing testing and extra language support. This support could include more one-on-one time talking and reading with the child. Use the strategies discussed in this chapter, and work closely with families to get a clear picture of the child's comprehension and language use. Your local early intervention (EI) program can provide support for children birth to 5 with language delays that includes their families and teachers. Find information on the Early Childhood Technical Assistance Center website: http://ectacenter.org/families.asp.

Autism Spectrum Disorder

Some children who experience language delays also exhibit challenges with social skills and behavior. They may make little eye contact, not respond to a parent's smile, have difficulty sharing in joint attention, repeat the same behaviors over and over, and have trouble adapting to changes in routines (CDC 2019). Physicians may identify toddlers and twos who exhibit these signs and others with autism spectrum disorder (ASD). Each child with ASD has different skills, strengths, and needs. If you notice that a child shows signs of ASD, involve your director to determine resources to share with the family so that they can obtain a free child- and family-centered assessment from your community's EI services program. Early diagnosis and assistance is important. If a child already identified with ASD is in your care, she may receive EI services.

Find information about your state's early intervention program at the CDC website (www.cdc.gov) and additional information about ASD from the National Institute of Mental Health (NIMH; www.nimh.nih.gov).

Learning to communicate effectively is one of the most important skills that children birth to 3 learn with you. Your thoughtful support of early language skills ensures that young children will be better language communicators and have larger vocabularies in the preschool years (Kim, Im, & Kwon 2015).

naeyc
Accreditation

This chapter supports the following NAEYC Early Learning Programs standards and topics

Program Standard 2: Curriculum
2.A Essential Characteristics
2.D Language Development
2.E Early Literacy

Chapter 6

The Wonder of Thinking and Learning

Infants and toddlers are taking in, digesting, and organizing information constantly. They are born with the capacity to be problem solvers extraordinaire and have an insatiable appetite for learning.

Cognitive development—learning, thinking, and problem solving—includes infants' and toddlers'

> Developing approaches to learning

> Imitating to learn and build relationships

> Developing executive functioning

> Gaining knowledge and applying it to solve problems and act creatively

Approaches to Learning

Children vary in the ways they respond to learning situations. Some easily take risks and approach new experiences and materials with enthusiasm; others tend to watch and enter a situation more slowly. The term *approaches to learning* describes these behaviors and attitudes. It includes curiosity, mastery motivation, and strategies for meeting goals.

Curiosity

Curiosity drives learning. When encouraged and supported, curiosity grows as infants and toddlers develop. The questions children ask, the problems they try to solve, and their sense of wonder provide multiple opportunities for teachers to support learning to learn.

Picture the older toddler who is curious about a new toy. The child can hardly wait to pick up the toy and examine all its fun and learning possibilities. If it is a plastic cup with two handles, the toddler might bang it, turn it upside down, shake it, look into it, and try to drink out of the cup. Support curiosity by recognizing its importance and encouraging children to explore objects safely. Say with true awe in your voice, "I wonder how that works." Or, with a surprised voice say, "Look at that truck go. What did you do to make it go so fast?" Model curiosity.

While most children will demonstrate curiosity, some children may observe more than experiment with objects. Other children may have been punished for exploring and are hesitant to do so in a new environment. They may need to learn to trust you and the safety of the situation before they express their curiosity and try different strategies to solve problems, such as how to move a noisy truck across the floor or pull a toy that has a safe rope as a handle. These children need your careful observation to determine what toys or materials will spark their interests.

Mastery Motivation

Most infants and toddlers have a desire to master tasks. Help them develop their sense of mastery by providing materials, such as puzzles, that are challenging but not too frustrating. Include puzzles of various levels—such as puzzle pieces with knobs on them and 1-piece, 2-piece, 10-piece, 20-piece, and some 30-piece puzzles for older toddlers. Thoughtful choices of materials allow children to pick what they feel comfortable doing.

Open-ended, creative materials also lend themselves to exploration. An older infant with a big, fat crayon makes marks on paper, a young toddler dabs at the paper and makes scribble lines, and older toddlers begin to make circles. They all may experiment with assorted colors. They master a task at their level, leaving them with a sense of accomplishment and a desire to do more. Your careful observation of each child gives you valuable information on what they might be ready to tackle next.

Goals, Theories, and Experimentation

Young children have goals and try different strategies to accomplish these goals. "Even in their earliest, most dependent days, babies' brains are pushing for understanding, trying to make sense of the world around them and the people in it" (Lally 2014, 4).

> With a determined look on his face, Joshua (8 months) tries to pick up the plastic bone on the end of a string attached to a toy dog on wheels. He finally grasps the bone and pulls on the string. He looks surprised when the dog rolls closer to him. He pulls harder on the bone, and the dog rolls quickly to him. He gleefully looks to his teacher to see if she is watching.

Joshua has a goal and figures out how to make it happen. He also wants to share his discovery with his teacher, whose attention means a great deal to him.

It is exciting to see a young toddler think up different strategies to solve a problem, as Kenyon does in the following example.

> Kenyon (14 months) rolls a ball under a couch in his family child care home. He first tries to retrieve the ball using his own body by lying on the floor and sticking his hands as far as he can under the couch. Then he toddles around the couch to see if the ball has come out on the other side. It has! As Kenyon picks up the ball, he beams, excited that he has figured out a solution to the problem.

At home, older toddlers might find a broom and use the handle to push the ball out from under the couch. If given opportunities in a safe environment, children will problem solve. You support experimentation when you do the following:

> Provide a variety of materials and toys that interest each child.

> Give children ample time to explore their environment.

> Observe a child's goals and the strategies used to accomplish these goals, for example, how they change their hand movements to roll a car across the floor or make water splash, and then provide more opportunities for the child to use those strategies.

> Notice if the child looks to you to celebrate an accomplishment, and then use specific words in an admiring tone to describe what the child just did—for example, "You jumped so high."

Infants and toddlers learn by watching; however, they learn more by doing (Bakker, Sommerville, & Gredebäck 2016). Young children must explore with their hands, mouths, feet, nose, and toes to learn.

Infants and toddlers develop theories about how people and objects work. These are ideas that they have developed themselves. They have wonderful ideas about how things work. No one tells them, "See, gravity causes objects to fall." Instead, they drop objects from different heights. They drop food from their plates to the floor. From these experiences, children begin to develop a *schema*—an idea about objects and how things work. Their theory is that when a person lets go of an object, it falls. Now, imagine their surprise when they first see a ball fall but then it bounces up again. When children encounter a situation that contradicts what they have come

to expect and understand, they must do what Piaget (1968) called *accommodate* their thinking. They must change their ideas and experiment further to see what falls and what flies, what bounces and what goes splat on the ground.

Watch for those moments when infants and toddlers furrow their brows or open their eyes wide in surprise. They are making discoveries. They are true scientists experimenting to see what will happen. Enjoy seeing them make discoveries, like trying to roll a square block after rolling a ball. The square block won't roll. The toddler may try again. She's learning something new. Young children are constantly making discoveries that no longer puzzle us as adults. As you share infants' and toddlers' excitement over their discoveries, you also are building emotional bonds with them. Young children's discoveries are much more fun and memorable for them when they are shared with you, who appreciates the joy of their learning.

Think about how you can challenge children's thinking in both big and small ways (see Chapter 11 for additional suggestions):

> Place a solid piece with other pieces that have holes in the middle with a stacking toy.

> Place a fuzzy toy in a sock with multiple solid toys.

> Read storybooks with pop-up pictures or hidden pictures that spark the interest of young children.

Infants and toddlers are constantly making theories about what you do, too. When they communicate to you that they need help, do you help them? When they express hunger, do you feed them? With each of your actions in response to their expressions of need, young children learn whether they can trust you or not.

Imitating to Learn and Build Relationships

Imitation is a powerful way that infants and toddlers learn. An 8-month-old gradually lifts her arms when a parent exclaims, "How big are you? So big!" while lifting his own arms. Fourteen-month-olds show *deferred imitation*. During the day a toddler might watch a friend give a peer who is crying a toy and then later in the day give a toy to his baby sister who is crying at home. The toddler can remember the behavior and imitate it later in the day or week.

> Rachel (12 months) watches as her teacher places a plastic blue ring on a stacking toy. The teacher then takes off the blue ring and places it on the floor. Rachel struggles but finally places the blue ring on the toy. Later in the day, the teacher notices Rachel placing the ring on the toy and then taking it off many times.

Infants and toddlers such as Rachel imitate to learn. Twelve-month-olds are more likely to imitate an adult who is reliable and whom they view as an expert. When 18-month-olds observed an adult say the incorrect name for objects that the toddlers knew, they were then less likely to imitate that unreliable person (Brooker & Poulin-Dubois 2013). Young children should find you to be a reliable adult!

Infants and toddlers also imitate for social reasons (Hilbrink et al. 2013; Over & Carpenter 2015). Imitation is a relationship builder. Shrieks of joy ring out when two toddlers share imitation jumping with each other. When a toddler imitates another toddler marching around, this helps cement their relationship. One toddler is feeling "I'm like you," and the other toddler is feeling "I like you." This type of imitation is a sort of social glue that connects people to each other (Hilbrink et al. 2013). Observe and deeply appreciate imitation as both a toddler learning and social strategy.

When you appreciate young children's imitation of you or peers, you support an important learning strategy and children's desire to connect emotionally with others.

You can encourage imitation by providing two of the same toy or musical instrument for children to discover as they sit by each other on the floor. You can encourage a toddler to imitate another toddler by saying, "Look at Sam jump. Do you want to jump with Sam?"

Developing Executive Functioning

By meeting young children's emotional needs for comfort and attention you also help them more effectively develop *executive functioning*—how to control their emotions and behavior in appropriate, healthy ways (self-regulate); focus on tasks; and use flexible thinking (Cuevas et al. 2014). We discussed self-regulation and its importance in Chapter 3. These executive functioning skills pave the way for children to learn, and they predict how well children will do academically in preschool and elementary school. They are related to children's present and future social success. For example, children who can attend for extended periods of time are more likely to be able to set goals, plan, and problem solve. This allows them to succeed in school and with friends (Zysset et al. 2018).

To adults, toddlers might seem to have short attention spans. Often, however, they focus intently and for extended periods of time on materials that interest them, as when they climb in a sandbox or begin to play with water. Give an older infant or toddler a toy bus with doors that open and shut and toy people that the child can place in seats on the bus. Many young children will focus for lengthy periods of time as they take the people out and put them back in their seats. They may open and shut the doors, pick the bus up and shake the people out, and then put the people back in again. Older toddlers may begin to pretend that the bus is broken and that they need to get a tow truck to pull the bus to a mechanic.

Researchers know that "infant attention span suffers when parents' eyes wander during playtime" (Yu & Smith 2016). If you are close by, a 1-year-old may expect you to be with her, paying attention, giving her eye contact when she looks up at you. We also know that some infants and toddlers need some time alone. They turn their backs to others in the room to experiment with nesting cups without interference from peers. Observe children's preferences, which may or may not change from day to day.

Executive functioning involves flexibility in thinking through a task. Think about the following toddler, who loves playdough.

> Mariana (30 months) loves the feel of playdough and uses her hands to punch it, pick it up and plop it down, and shape it into balls and long cylinder worms. Sometimes, if a teacher is not looking, she tastes it! She then goes outside and plays with sand and tries to roll the sand, punch it, pick it up and plop it down, and shape it into balls. She finds that she must change how she interacts with sand. She must be flexible in her thinking. She looks around and sees a cup and pail. She scoops up the sand in her cup and dumps it in the bucket.

Day to Day the Relationship Way

Realizing that sand acts differently from playdough, Mariana changes both her goals and her strategies to play successfully with sand. She demonstrates flexibility in thinking.

Be emotionally available as infants and toddlers play. Offer encouragement and specific comments about what they are doing. Provide plenty of time for them to explore a rich personal and physical environment, experiencing a variety of materials, equipment, and people.

What Infants and Toddlers Are Learning

Infants and toddlers are discovering so much in the early years. They are learning about object permanence, cause-and-effect relationships, math and science concepts, reading (early literacy skills), and symbols, and that others have minds.

Learning About Object Permanence

Infants and toddlers are learning that objects exist permanently in space and time. Their stuffed dog disappears when covered by a blanket. However, it still exists. Piaget (1954) discovered that infants do not look for an object that an adult hides, under a pillow for example, until around 8 to 9 months of age. However, new methods of research show that infants realize that a hidden object should continue to exist by 6 months of age. For example, when researchers hid a disc and a triangle behind a screen, when the researchers lifted the screen and both shapes were gone, the infants were surprised and looked at the scene longer (Kibbe & Leslie 2011). The infants seemed to realize that objects should continue to exist.

Older infants will begin to look over the side of their high chair when they drop a piece of food to see if it still exists when out of sight for a moment. Older infants and young toddlers may even test their theory that objects continue to exist by hiding their toys and then looking to see if they are still there. They may play a game of throwing an object and the adult retrieving it over and over. Use spatial language such as "Where did the ball go? Oh, the ball is *under* the blanket," while lifting up the blanket and pointing to the ball. Provide containers of a variety of sizes and shapes so that infants and toddlers experiment with dropping objects in them, looking to see if the objects are in the container, and then retrieving the objects.

Learning About Cause-and-Effect Relationships

Infants experiment with cause-and-effect relationships. Three-month-olds learn to shake their foot to ring a bell safely sewn on an elastic band around their ankle, and 6-month-olds experiment with how to move their hands differently to make a cylinder roll or to pick up a toy. Toddlers are scientists, trying to figure out how everything works.

To encourage children's learning experiments, offer children acceptable items for experimenting with cause and effect—toys they can make move, items that produce a noise, or materials they can change in some way. Observe when infants and toddlers repeat an action to get an effect. A young infant bats at a toy, watches it swing, and then bats it again. Toddlers become true experimenters who try several ways to make a truck move. Toddlers may turn the truck over and over looking for buttons to push to turn a toy on to make a sound. Musical toys, toys with safe buttons to push, blocks that stick together, sand toys—some with an opening on the bottom so that sand falls out—and water toys all encourage children to explore cause-and-effect relationships.

Learning About Math

Children develop math concepts and skills early in life. From the moment they are born, infants begin to form mathematical ideas through everyday experiences and their interactions with trusted adults. Math language—how you talk with infants and toddlers about math ideas like *more*, *empty*, and *full*—matters (NAEYC n.d. b). As Greenberg (2012, 62) explains, "Math is all around us; math talk brings it out and makes it known."

Learning about numbers. Play and adult talk about numbers are the ways for children to gain *number sense*. *Number* represents quantity—how many of something there is—while the word *numeral* represents the symbols we use to indicate how many—1, 2, 3, and so on. Talking about numbers begins early with infants and is a natural part of their daily routines and interactions with you. You might say,

> "You have *two* hands."

> "How *many* peas are there? Let's count, one, two, three."

> "You ate *all* of your applesauce. It is *all gone*."

> Rafaella, (11 months) focuses intently on picking up her mashed peas off her tray with her fingers. After she finishes, she looked up at her mother and signs "more" by placing the fingers of her two hands together in the middle of her body. Rafaella understands that when she uses the sign language for "more," her mother brings her more peas.

Rafaella understands the mathematical concept of "more." Learning the names of the numerals is more difficult for toddlers than learning about the concept of number. Rather than quizzing children, we help by naming the numerals often when we see them in the environment or in books. Many children's books include the numeral by the number of objects on the page. For example, Eric Carle's book *1, 2, 3 to the Zoo: A Counting Book* includes a numeral on each page. You can say, "Look, here is the numeral 1," as you point to it. "Oh, look, there is one elephant."

Learning about shapes and spatial relationships. Infants and toddlers learn about how objects and persons—including their own bodies—fit into different spaces. They may try to squeeze through an opening between two toy shelves that teachers have anchored safely so as not to fall over. Toddlers will crawl through play tunnels and try to fit as many objects as possible into a play purse. Encourage children's understanding by using spatial words to describe the direction and position of objects when children are eating or playing. For example,

> "Look, Jax put his napkin under his plate!"

> "Carlos, your doll is next to David's doll."

Use words such as *circle*, *triangle*, *bent*, *edge*, and *corner*. As you hold up a cracker during snack, say, "Look, this cracker is square. Let's count how many sides it has" (as you point to each side and count). Use words that represent spatial understandings, such as *up*, *down*, *over*, *around*, and *through*, often during children's play. When toddlers use these words, reinforce their use by responding, repeating the words, and possibly showing the contrasting term. For example, if a toddler exclaims, "The ball went *up*," say, "Yes, the ball went up when you threw it. And then the ball came *down*!" These words promote children's understanding of where objects are in space. Toddlers and preschool children from 14 to 46 months of age use more spatial terms if their teachers use such terms when talking with the children (NSF 2011).

Observe how young children explore spatial relationships. Building with blocks and playing with puzzles support the understanding of how objects fit in space. Provide infants and toddlers opportunities to fill different size containers with objects, play with stacking ring toys and cups that nest inside others, and crawl through cloth tunnels. These spatial explorations relate to children's later mathematical skills (Verdine et al. 2014).

Learning about classification and seriation. Infants and toddlers begin to *classify*, or sort objects and people according to their characteristics. For example, they decide which foods they like and which they do not like. Children will use the skills of seeing similarities and differences in objects and grouping them throughout their life. Matching and comparing objects, toys, and pictures are skills that lead to children sorting objects by color, shape, or type of animal. Toddlers may be able to sort items by one dimension, such as color—placing the blue blocks in one pile and the red blocks in another pile. When you use words such as *heavier*, *lighter*, *rougher*, *smoother*, and *bumpier*, you are helping them notice differences in objects.

Seriation is the process of arranging objects in order by characteristics, such as length or width. Young children will use the skill of recognizing differences in sizes and arranging objects in order by size as they play, eat, and learn to count. When you say, "Look, this dog is the *biggest*. This dog is the *smallest*," when comparing different toy dogs, you are seriating. Words like *large*, *larger*, *largest*; *small*, *smaller*, *smallest*; *tall*, *taller*, *tallest*; and *short*, *shorter*, *shortest* help young children learn to order items according to size, length, or width.

Learning About Science

Infants and toddlers are natural researchers and scientists. That is why toddlers unroll toilet paper and follow bugs across the playground. Young children are curious. They observe living things, the properties of objects and materials, and people. They ask questions. They make guesses as to why people, animals, objects, materials, the sun, and so on act as they do. They experiment to test whether their guesses are correct. Observing, asking questions, making guesses, experimenting, and drawing conclusions is what science is for infants and toddlers.

> Kai (2 years) notices an ant carrying a bread crumb across the playground. He and his teacher follow it for about 30 minutes, taking care not to step on the ant. They wonder together where that ant is going and how much it can carry. Later, after everyone is inside, the teacher finds a book on ants that she places on the science table. The next day the teacher and Kai look at the book together.

Encourage children's curiosity and exploration. Be present with young children. Notice what they are investigating with their senses. Notice how they repeat actions on objects—shaking, banging, throwing, and bouncing them to learn their properties and what they can do. Observe how infants and toddlers respond to wind, water, blocks, and beads. Notice how they love watching the way water flows through a hole in the bottom of a used orange juice can. Encourage them to feel the coldness of snow and the wetness of water with their fingers. Use language to describe in detail what they are thinking and doing. Continually wonder with them. You support infant or toddler scientists as you explore the world with them!

Following are some ways to encourage toddlers' curiosity, exploration, and problem solving:

⟩ Provide objects that sink and float in the water table. Encourage toddlers to guess which ones will sink and which will float.

⟩ Provide a ramp or plank. Encourage toddlers to experiment with how fast different items will roll down the ramp. Adjust the ramp's height and incline. Wonder with the children why some items go faster than others.

⟩ Provide opportunities for toddlers to mix colors together on paper with paint brushes. Talk about the colors as children create them.

⟩ Cook with toddlers. Notice and wonder with them how ingredients change when they are mixed and cooked.

These activities encourage science learning.

Learning About Symbols and Dramatic Play

Infants and toddlers progress through stages in their *symbolic play*. In this activity young children use objects or actions to represent other objects and actions. They pretend. For example, you have probably seen a young toddler pretend to drink from a cup or eat with a spoon—familiar actions. Next, older toddlers may pretend using familiar actions, but using them with objects, such as dolls. They may pretend to brush the doll's hair or pretend to feed the doll.

Two-year-olds begin *dramatic play*. They pretend that they are someone else, for example, the mommy or daddy. They often shift very quickly, though, to be a dog or kitty. They still need props that are realistic, such as pretend dishes that look like dishes, and then they soon advance to using props that do not look like the object they represent. They are learning to think more abstractly when the pretend item looks less like the real item. For example, an older 2-year-old might use a piece of straw that he finds outside to represent an ice cream cone.

Symbolic play provides a foundation for learning to read. A straw doesn't look like an ice cream cone, and the letters *d-u-c-k* do not look like a duck. During play, children learn that one object can represent another, just as letters represent a word and an object.

Symbolic and dramatic play enhance learning about themselves and others. Young children need many opportunities to participate in symbolic play and dramatic play to experiment with who they are and act out their beliefs and feelings.

Engage in symbolic play with infants and toddlers. Here are some ways to support it:

⟩ Build on toddlers' ideas. For example, drink many cups of pretend juice, thanking the toddler and adding novel words by commenting on the delicious flavor of the juice. Encourage the toddler to offer "juice" to other toddlers who are nearby to include them in the play.

⟩ Enthusiastically engage with the toddler and expand on the symbolic play. If, for example, a toddler "mommy" or "daddy" is pushing a doll in a small buggy and is going "shopping," you can quickly set up a "store" with cardboard boxes and pretend they are groceries. As you are playing, you are modeling language and encouraging the development of a story line. Include other children by asking the "shopper" if she wants a friend to go shopping with her.

> Continually think about how you can include more toddlers in the play by asking or commenting on a pretending toddler's need for a "baby," "checker at the grocery store," or "firefighter."

> Most importantly, if toddlers are directing their own play, stand back and observe whether you could provide more props (boxes, chairs, dolls, doll beds, blankets, etc.) to expand their play.

Learning About Others' Minds

Theory of mind is a term used to describe the ability of one person to think about what another person is thinking. This develops slowly over the first three years. Before 18 months of age, most toddlers will give goldfish crackers to an adult researcher, even though the adult has indicated that she likes broccoli best. Because toddlers love goldfish crackers so much, they give them to the broccoli-loving adult. After approximately 18 months, toddlers will give broccoli to the adult who indicates a preference for broccoli. The toddlers are taking the perspective of others. The toddlers think about the preference of the adult—even though the adult's desires are different from their own (Repacholi & Gopnik 1997).

Help infants and toddlers develop the ability to take the perspective of another person. When reading a story to toddlers about a boy who hurts his hand, say, "Look at the boy's face. He is feeling so sad. Do you think he wants a hug?"

Keep in mind that even though young children are just beginning to know another's mind, they read and react to the *emotions* of others. For example, in one research study 7-month-old infants looked attentively at adults' fearful facial expressions and their heart rate decreased, which also indicated heightened attention (Peltola et al. 2015). These infants most likely did not understand why the adults had fearful faces, but they were sensitive to the emotional expressions.

Facilitating Cognitive Development

The *zone of proximal development* (Vygotsky 1978) is the learning area between what an infant or toddler does independently and what she achieves with the support of an adult or more skilled peer. One key to facilitating learning within the zone of proximal development is to scaffold learning. *Scaffolding* is a widely used term to describe the responsive support that adults use to help children learn at a higher level than if they were playing by themselves (Brownfield & Wilkinson 2018). For example, Lorenzo, 18 months old, expertly places blocks in a container with a wide opening. He cannot, however, place shapes in a container with an opening that is just the size of the shape. By suggesting a strategy for Lorenzo to use to succeed with that task, his teacher scaffolds his learning. She might model how to hold the shape in such a way that it drops in the hole or ask Lorenzo if he wants help. If he nods his head or says, "Help," the teacher might guide his hand to hold the shape in a successful way. The teacher is providing the child tools or strategies to be successful.

Watching a child struggle, for example, when trying to place one block on top of another, is often difficult, but it is important to give the child ample time to try to succeed. If given time, with you emotionally present, the child may try several strategies to create a tower. He will build his own toolkit of strategies and learn to see himself as a competent persistent solver of problems.

However, if the child becomes frustrated with a task, it is time to scaffold his learning. Watching the child's face and body posture will tell you a great deal about how he is feeling.

Cognitive Challenges

Some children experience delays in their reasoning, memory, and problem-solving skills. If you suspect a delay, begin by individualizing your response to the child and observe closely. Try the following strategies:

> Help the child feel safe so that he or she can focus on learning.

> Continually observe the child's interests and provide your enthusiastic responses and materials to fuel the learning spark.

> Notices the strategies that the child uses to explore objects—such as banging, turning objects over, putting objects in and out of containers, stringing large beads—and then provide more materials that engage him or her.

> Break down tasks into parts so the child can be successful. For example, give the child 10 blocks to use to experiment with rather than 100 or repeat two lines of a song rather than the whole song to help the child learn to sing it.

> Comment on effort and strategies, not outcome. For example, say, "You are turning the toy over and over," and "You are working so hard." And instead of saying, "Good boy" and "Great," say, "You pulled the string. What happened?"

Make sure to document your observations and your actions.

As you build an even closer relationship with the child, you may determine that it's appropriate to talk with the family about the free assessments provided by your local early intervention services program. Coordinate with your director and make sure to provide the family with details of your individualization and observations.

Young children's cognitive development depends on an enriched personal and physical environment with strong relationships. Celebrate their new accomplishments with them!

This chapter supports the following NAEYC Early Learning Programs standards and topics

Program Standard 2: Curriculum
2.A Essential Characteristics
2.F Early Mathematics
2.G Science
2.H Technology

Chapter 7

The Wonder of Learning to Move Successfully

Each day we marvel at how quickly infants and toddlers learn to move their fingers, hands, arms, legs, and toes in different ways. We know that most young children are naturally driven to move. We also know that our emotional and physical presence supports young children's motivation to learn to use their small and large muscles and their enjoyment in accomplishing new motor milestones. Our smiles at a surprised infant who turns over for the first time helps him relax and enjoy the moment. Our enthusiastic support of an older infant who attempts to walk lets the infant know we share her excitement and will keep her safe. When we share the exuberance of older toddlers when they run, jump, stack blocks, and climb, we build their confidence and their delight in their accomplishments.

Learning to move successfully is an important part of children effectively and confidently participating in both relationships and the environment as they develop.

Young children are developing their

> Fine motor skills (use of hands, toes, face, and eyes)

> Large motor skills (use of arms and legs)

> Balance and coordination

> Sensory skills including vision, hearing, smelling, tasting, and touch

Developing Fine Motor Skills

Small muscle development (fine motor skills) includes the muscles of eyes, hands, fingers, feet, and toes. Early on, infants turn their eyes to follow an interesting toy that you move slowly either horizontally or vertically in front of their face. By 4 months their eyes can even follow a circular motion of that toy.

At about 5 months, infants use a raking motion with all their fingers to bring a toy or some food on a tabletop toward themselves. Eight-month-olds begin, with the support of the other three fingers, to use mostly the pads of their forefinger and thumb (*inferior pincer grasp*) to pick up objects. Triumphantly using only the thumb and forefinger (*superior pincer prehension*), 1-year-olds pick up pieces of food to feed themselves. They also may pick up tiny pieces of dust or lint from the floor and pop them in their mouths (just another reason to be careful in making sure infants are moving in a clean, safe environment).

If offered a set of cubes on a tabletop, a year-old infant, regardless of hand maturity, may pick one up with vigor, only to drop it on the floor. The infant then practices this newly perfected skill on the next block in the pile. Lots of blocks end up on the floor—a testimony to the rapid development of excellent prehension skills. Be proud of your patience and even feelings of amusement at seeing the child practice this "task" with quick, deft hand motions.

Facial muscle control evolves more slowly. Infants cannot manage until the middle of the first year to close their lips firmly while eating, which explains the food dribbles seen from the corners of their mouths!

Wrist control is usually complete between 18 months and 2 years of age. If an infant acts frustrated while trying to tip a cup far enough toward her mouth to get a sip of water, gently guide her hands to help. A toddler may pick up a cup to drink and suddenly juice is spilling all over. Sippy cups are helpful, and providing a two-handled cup challenges a toddler to practice wrist control skills. Toddlers need these skills to lift a spoon with food on it and direct it toward their mouth. Expect many spills to occur as toddlers develop their wrist control.

By 18 months toddlers are beginning to become skilled builders, controlling their eyes and hands together to place one block on top of another. They love to stack large cardboard blocks.

Yet toddlers may still have trouble assessing block size. Suppose a toddler places a larger block on top of a smaller one over and over. Each time the larger block topples over. Frustrating! After a while, the perceptive teacher models placing a larger block underneath a smaller one. Or the adult gently asks the toddler: "What if you put the largest block on the bottom first?"

By 2 years, toddlers grasp crayons (fat ones are easier to hold) with a firm grip and make lines on a page. They pick up pieces of a puzzle and begin to learn to turn the pieces to fit. By 3 years, children are making big circles with a crayon on paper.

From reaching to bat or swipe at a mobile to manipulating small objects proficiently, infants' and toddlers' small motor development flourishes. You provide both the physical materials and the children's sense of security to explore an interesting environment. It is your affection, emotionally supportive presence, and creation of developmentally appropriate experiences that support young children's desire to use their small muscles to learn and engage with others.

Developing Large Motor Skills

Large motor skills develop in an orderly way from head to toe. Newborns turn their heads, follow an object with their eyes, and kick their legs. As infants spend time on their tummies, they begin to lift their chests and heads. Given many opportunities to move, 4-month-olds roll from tummy to back. Many infants sit sturdily between 6 and 8 months. Others need more time to gain muscular control, and they topple slowly forward when placed in a sitting position. By 7 months you may see a motivated infant lift her body on all fours and rock back and forth in anticipation of crawling.

Many infants delight in crawling. Others become frustrated as they try hard to coordinate their limbs. They try, try, and try again. Some creep with their bottoms in the air. Others slide on their tummies and then master the crawl. Some start out by crawling backward. Enjoy watching these styles for each infant in your care. Each child's actions may be different, but most children want to move.

By one year, infants are often ready to pull up to stand while grasping and holding on to firm, sturdy furniture. Learning body balance takes time! Walking around objects while holding on leads to that next brave moment when the older infant or young toddler lets go and ventures out into the world. Wobbly at first, toddlers walk with legs far apart. Soon they toddle with more and more confidence, intent on moving as fast as they can.

Toddlers begin to walk between 8 months and 20 months, with an average of 12 months. Children between 12 and 19 months old averaged 2,368 steps and 17 falls per hour (Adolph et al. 2012). Walking develops at various times for different children and has no relationship to intelligence (Jenni et al. 2013). There can be a 12-month difference between early and late walkers.

Some children watch their peers walk for weeks before walking themselves. Other children persist at trying to walk even though they stumble and fall. Newly walking infants can walk as much as the length of 37 football fields in a day and fall often (Adolph et al. 2012). No one needs to tell them or help them practice; most toddlers have an inner drive that pushes them to move. Your job is to appreciate the power of movement and provide opportunities, safe environments, and interesting goals that impel children to move to explore.

Learning Balance and Coordination

They are so determined to move, many infants who plop on their bottoms while trying to walk just get themselves up and go onward. When some young toddlers fall over as they are first trying to walk or trying to go faster, they might look to see how you are reacting. Remain calm and attentive, gently nod, and give encouragement. With this support, children are likely to get up and keep on trying, although some may need your reassuring hug or pat before they move forward to continue practicing their exhilarating new mobility.

As they develop more balance and coordination, toddlers become increasingly able to trot briskly around a corner without taking a tumble. They learn to walk without falling over even when they bend down to pick up a favorite toy they spy on the floor during a walk. As you witness each stage of increasing competence, you can be assured that the toddlers' secure relationship with you helps give them courage and confidence in their persistence to master locomotive skills.

Gaining Sensory Skills

Infants' and toddlers' sensory skills support their development of rich relationships with you and others as they see, hear, smell, taste, and touch you and the important people in their lives. When sensory skills are developing well, infants and toddlers are using their senses constantly to learn about and enjoy their environment.

Vision

Infants' vision is fuzzy during the first weeks (Dewar, n.d.). During the first four months, however, vision improves. With time, infants recognize your face and voice, and as you respond to their needs, they gain enough trust to feel comfortable draping on your shoulder or across your lap. Around 8 weeks, infants' ability to see color improves.

By 12 months of age, a child's vision is like an adult's. However, children are still learning to coordinate their eyes, hands, and movements together. You help children coordinate their movements and understand what they see when you richly describe their actions and enthusiastically share their excitement when they point at an object or person.

Hearing

Hearing is almost fully developed by birth; however, there still may be fluid in a newborn's middle ear. Infants will startle if there is a loud noise. They often quiet if they hear your calm voice. By 4 months of age, they look toward a new sound, and by 7 months will respond to their name. They begin to imitate sounds that they hear frequently. Keep the infant room free of excess sound, such as loud music playing all day. You and infants and toddlers thrive in an environment where people easily can hear each other talk and sing.

Hearing is critical for language development. Newborns are frequently tested now in hospitals across the United States. Yet infants and toddlers may still develop hearing challenges during the first three years. If there is any question about a child's hearing, encourage the family to talk with their child's doctor. You may notice that an infant doesn't startle when she hears a loud sound or a toddler doesn't seem to hear you unless the child is looking directly at your face and mouth. When hearing challenges are detected early and intervention begins, children's communication skills are more likely to develop normally.

Smells and Tastes

Newborns are highly sensitive to smell. Infants may be calmed by the smell of their mother's scarf; holding that scarf next to you sometimes works wonders to sooth an upset infant you are holding. Newborns prefer sweet tastes, which is why they like breast milk. They typically reject bitter or sour tastes (Kapsimali & Barlow 2013). If breastfed, infants learn to like the flavors of the fruits and vegetables that their mothers eat (Beauchamp & Mennella 2011). When infants in your program begin eating solid food, they may prefer those that they experienced in their mothers' breast milk. Toddlers' sense of smell helps them form memories. Savor smells together, such as the fragrance of fresh oranges at snack time or flowers on the playground. Describe them in detail so toddlers learn to connect the sensations with words for them.

A toddler's temperament may influence whether a child approaches or withdraws from new foods (Moding & Stifter 2018). Some toddlers exuberantly will dive into a new food. However, toddlers who are more cautious initially may reject a new food. If you continue to offer the rejected food, toddlers will often try it eventually (Forestell & Mennella 2007). When you have a caring relationship with a toddler, the toddler is more likely to trust you and imitate you as you try a new food and say, "Yum, that tastes good."

Touch

Loving touches are critical to infant well-being and enhance brain development (Dempsey-Jones 2017; Dewar, n.d.). You will figure out what kind of touch comforts each child. Does the infant like you to hold her firmly, or does she like gentle caresses on the arm? Young infants need to be held often during the day and for feeding time.

Busy toddlers may race to get a hug from you and then run off quickly to play, restored with emotional energy. But many still like to be held at times. Provide plenty of cuddles, caresses, and hugs during the day. At nap time, use gentle back pats to help children settle into sleep if they need it. Touch that is responsive to children's needs facilitates their healthy emotional and social development.

Facilitating Motor Development

Ensure that infants and toddlers feel secure and feel safe to move. *Felt security* is a young child's feeling that she is safe to explore away from a primary caregiver, trusting that the adult will be emotionally available when she needs attention. Observe for the beginnings of new skills. For example, when an infant can reach out to grasp objects, provide interesting objects to encourage her to reach and grasp. Infants and toddlers need space and opportunities to practice new moves such as pulling to stand, walking around sturdy objects while holding on, or learning to jump down from low objects. Young children need you to enjoy moving with them. They want you to experience delight with them when they master a new motor skill. Appreciate children's accomplishments with your enthusiastic specific comments: "You are walking. You jumped. You love to swing [sitting in a safe toddler seat on a swing set]."

Provide rocking boats that promote balancing skills and ability to coordinate large muscle activity with another toddler. Provide a set of safe steps so that toddlers safely practice climbing skills. Make sure there are mats below so that a child who tumbles is cushioned by a thick, soft surface beneath those few steps. Provide climbing bars for toddlers to swing from and develop sturdy shoulder and arm muscles.

Provide slides so that toddlers can learn to take turns, struggle up the stairs, and slide down. Give them opportunities when others are not using the slide to try to walk up the slide, as so many toddlers valiantly try to do once they have mastered sliding down.

Provide interesting visual experiences while facilitating motor development by taking children outdoors to see flowers, rocks, snails, ants, and other bugs on walks. Let them roll around on the grass and run around tree trunks. Provide a closely supervised shallow pool in warm weather so children feel warm water, wiggle their toes, and splash about safely. In crisp, chilly weather, dress toddlers warmly and let them run around, enjoy snow, and play chasing games. Provide objects that can be moved by toddlers, such as small tires, large and small pieces of cardboard, and wagons. Toddlers will use their large and small muscles as they play and create with these materials.

As they develop these skills, infants and toddlers look to you to

> Be a secure base from which they can explore and then come back to for emotional strength

> Set up a safe, fun, and developmentally appropriate environment for them to explore

> Be patient with their use of utensils to eat—fine motor skills are just developing in the first three years

> Be present and share the joy of new milestones, such as walking or picking up small items with their fingers

> Help "just enough" to help a discouraged child learn a strategy to accomplish a goal, such as climbing up the steps of a toddler slide

Sensory Challenges

Some infants and toddlers have sensory challenges. They may be sensitive to noises, too much visual stimulation, or certain types of touches. Or they may crave physical contact and other types of stimulation. A toddler may be cranky because the touch of the tag on his new T-shirt irritates his skin, or he may fuss if he sees foods touching each other on his plate. Another toddler may put his hands over his ears and become very distressed when other children squeal with joy as they chase each other. That child is extremely sensitive to loud, high-pitched sounds. Touch may cause discomfort or even pain for some children.

Your keen observations and discussions with families will help you sensitively respond with both personal and physical environmental adaptations for children. When your touch or other sensory input matches a child's needs in that moment, you are in tune with the child and are helping to reduce her stress levels (Feldman, Singer, & Zagoory 2010). Each child communicates the type of touch she needs. Some infants and toddlers snuggle into your arms and want firm hugs. Others may sit by your leg when you are sitting on the floor and just want to lean on you.

Some toddlers need to rub a special blanket or soft cloth doll against their cheeks for comfort when worried and trying to get calm. Observe each child closely so that you are aware of the toddler who self-soothes and tries to regain control of negative emotions this way rather than having a meltdown.

The challenge for families and teachers is to become tuned in to responses that signal that a child may have a particular sensory need and require special attention to feel physically better and emotionally understood. Encourage families to work closely with their child's doctor to determine the cause of sensory challenges.

You may think that infants and toddlers will gain their motor milestones and skills even without the support of caring adults. However, adult support is critical to children's successful motor development. Sometimes children feel frustrated, bewildered, tired, and tuned out from group activities, or they get discouraged when faced with new developmental challenges, such as using their fine muscles to eat more neatly or figuring out how to put together a new puzzle. Infants and toddlers need you to be a secure base, be patient, be present, and help "just enough."

This chapter supports the following NAEYC Early Learning Programs standards and topics

Program Standard 2: Curriculum
2.A Essential Characteristics
2.C Physical Development
2.K Health and Safety

Developing a Responsive, Relationship-Based Program

Part 3 highlights ways you can support children's development and learning through relationship-based interactions and program planning. Chapter 8 stresses your critical role as a relationship-based teacher, as you reflect, observe, and facilitate learning. Chapter 9 gives detailed information on how to create relationship-based environments and responsive learning opportunities. Chapter 10 discusses routines and relationships and opportunities for interactions and learning during each part of the program day. Chapter 11 defines curriculum for infants and toddlers, emphasizing observation and documentation of children's interests and learning to facilitate planning in a responsive way. Chapter 12 focuses on the importance of providing opportunities for infants and toddlers to sing, play with musical instruments, and listen to and explore books. Chapter 13 describes positive guidance strategies for building strong, caring relationships with children and families.

Chapter 8

A Responsive, Relationship-Based Teacher

A relationship-based teacher supports engaging, rewarding, positive, and healthy relationships with and between children and families in the program. These connections enable children to feel safe and to learn successfully. Responsive teachers respond gently to children's emotional cues, are sensitive and attuned to children's needs, and respond to children's learning initiatives by being quietly present, encouraging effort, providing language support, and sparking curiosity. Wondering how to respond is important; you wonder and try different strategies to see which ones best support each child's learning needs. Being physically and emotionally present aids children in their efforts and in feeling good about their accomplishments.

A responsive, relationship-based teacher considers

> How to be a reflective practitioner

> How to be a collaborator with children to facilitate learning

> How to be a keeper of the spirit of the child

Be a Reflective Practitioner

Reflective practice is a key component of being a relationship-based, responsive teacher. Reflective practitioners think deeply and deliberately about their practices and how these influence children, families, and co-teachers.

Reflective teachers

> Consider how their practice can be developmentally appropriate and effective

> Promote equity and inclusion with children and families

> Continually consider how their own identities and biases influence their behavior

> Seek to understand how children's personalities and behaviors influence how they interact with children

Use Developmentally Appropriate Practice

"Developmentally appropriate practice (DAP) is an approach to teaching grounded in the research on how young children develop and learn and in what is known about effective early education" (NAEYC n.d. a). DAP includes age appropriate, individually appropriate, and culturally appropriate interactions, environments, and learning opportunities.

Age appropriateness. This component is research based and involves knowing about child development and learning. Children of different ages typically need distinct kinds of care. Infants need close bodily contact, feeding on demand, and time to both engage in interaction and sleep peacefully when they are tired. They also need safe toys and books that they explore while being held in a teacher's lap or while the educators are close by, sitting on the floor. Young toddlers need teachers who recognize their need for attention and who provide many opportunities for long explorations of interesting indoor and outdoor environments. Children will toddle back to teachers for emotional refueling, gaining back an adventurous spirit. They need teachers who are emotionally available. Those working with older toddlers recognize children's need for autonomy—for making decisions about *where*, with *whom*, and *how* they play.

Children of all ages need adults who share their curiosity and delight in new experiences; understand the importance of stable and secure loving relationships for young children; know how to support children's emotional, social, language, thinking, and movement development; and can identify when children need additional support to achieve learning goals.

Individual appropriateness and children's uniqueness. Each child has similar needs and yet is so different from other children. One infant is content to explore the materials right around him, so you provide many objects within reach that are safe to grasp and check in with him occasionally as you play games with another infant who needs to interact with you. One toddler loves moving, so you offer opportunities and space for her to toddle fast, push trucks across the floor or outdoors, climb, swing, and jump. For an older toddler who likes to concentrate on fitting puzzle pieces into the correct spaces, you quietly allow space and time for him to do so, providing more challenging puzzles for that toddler as appropriate. Another toddler babbles at every picture in a story, prompting you to fit in time to snuggle with her and her favorite books.

Cultural and linguistic diversity. The term *culture* refers to a way of life (Rothman 2014). Culture has a powerful influence on how children feel and learn. Learn about each child's culture by conversing with their families. For example, a family might greatly value children's interdependence, encouraging reliance on family members and close-knit relationships at home. Other families may encourage their children to be more independent, to play longer by themselves, and to look to themselves as well as others for affirmation and feelings of success.

When families feel that a program respects diverse cultures and families, they may feel more comfortable talking with you about their customs, beliefs, family lives, and goals for their children. As a result, families may come to trust your practices with their children even if they differ from the families' own ways. Unless home practices are harmful, such as the use of physical punishment, strive to respect what families desire for their children. Listen when there are different approaches or even disagreements, try to understand all viewpoints, and work together to find acceptable solutions.

Supporting the home languages of children and helping them learn a new language in the program setting are both vital to dual language learners' development and relationships. Look for ways to implement the curriculum so that it "reflects the family values, beliefs, experiences, cultures, and languages of all enrolled children" (NAEYC 2018, 21). For example, learn some words in a child's home language if you do not speak it, seek out interpreters if necessary for you to communicate with families, and show families that you respect them.

Reflect on the Importance of Equity and Inclusion

Reflective teachers promote fairness and impartiality in all their interactions (NAEYC 2018). What does this mean for day-to-day practice? It means that you

> Treat each child and family member with kindness and respect

> Welcome families of all cultures and ethnicities, family structures, and practices

> Treat all children and families equitably, including children with disabilities

The term *inclusion* refers to ensuring that children with identified disabilities can participate as fully as possible in a program alongside their peers who do not have disabilities. Inclusion benefits both the infant or toddler with a delay or disability and children without delays or disabilities. Children with disabilities imitate and learn from other children. They often try walking and talking like their peers. With teacher support, children without identified disabilities learn to be comfortable with, for example, a child who uses adaptive equipment. They learn that children with disabilities like many of the same things that they like.

Responsive teachers build on each child's individual strengths, needs, and interests. It is important, though, to ask for ongoing assistance from a special educator and other specialists to meet the needs of all the children in the program and to help you know how best to help the child with disabilities and others in the program.

The Influence of Your Own and Children's Cultures, Beliefs, and Behaviors

Children differ in ethnicity, gender, family experiences, and the languages they speak. Reflect on how your own culture and beliefs influence how you interact with children who may differ from you.

Children also differ in behavior. Think about child behaviors that make you feel sad, angry, or frustrated. Everyone has different experiences that affect how they feel about certain behaviors. You may delight in a child who is boisterous, funny, and engaging, whereas another teacher may find this child exhausting. Your experiences, culture, and beliefs about children influence how you feel about their behavior and how you feel, react, and behave with them. Reflective practitioners continually examine their reactions to each child. If you find yourself wanting to spend less time with a child, think about why you feel this way. If you often feel irritated with a certain child, consider what you can change. Infants and toddlers with more challenging temperaments—like all children—need your sincere attempts to provide loving interactions and responses in order to thrive.

Infants and toddlers feel and need your appreciation and admiration for their uniqueness—their abilities, gender, strengths, needs, cultures, and languages.

Be a Responsive Facilitator of Learning

A facilitator of children's learning organizes experiences, encourages curiosity and discovery, and scaffolds children's learning. Think of yourself as a responsive, warm, creative guide who

> Is emotionally available to children

> Gives children wholehearted and kindly attention (sometimes just by your presence)

> Creates possibilities for learning that are age, individually, and culturally appropriate and effective

> Provides ample time for infants and toddlers to explore their environments each day, making choices, and building their initiative and motivation to learn

> Observes thoughtfully while an infant or toddler explores a toy, noticing a child's goals and strategies, and not interrupting a child's engaged problem solving

> Observes children's interests and goals (e.g., how different materials sound when dropped) and changes your interactions with them and the environment as needed to spark learning and curiosity

> Warmly *responds* when a child wants or needs you, looks at you, verbalizes to you, or needs you to be close

> Engages in rich language conversations with infants and toddlers and gives them time to respond

> Uses language to describe what children are doing (parallel talk) and what you are doing (self-talk)

> Wonders with children as they play or as you read a book

> Supports (scaffolds) learning by helping children learn strategies before they become frustrated

> Facilitates just enough to help the child feel confident enough to try again

> Encourages a child's effort by offering comments such as "You are working so hard to turn the pages of the book! You can see each baby animal."

You are an educator who is *response-able* (Cheeseman 2017). This means that you are ready to respond when infants and toddlers initiate an exchange. For example, if a toddler holds out a plastic fruit for you to see, you might respond in one of the following ways, depending on your knowledge of the child:

> Smile and provide the name of the fruit: "I see! You have an apple."

> Talk about what the child was doing with the fruit—shaking, banging, making noise, trying to make it do something, or pretending to eat or cook with it.

> Describe the fruit—for example, its color, shape, size, or length.

> Suggest something the child might do with the fruit.

> Say, "What would you like to do with the apple?"

Understand the Importance of Play

Play is the way children learn (Gillespie 2016). The commonly heard saying that "play is children's work" highlights the importance of taking play seriously. Imaginative, creative, purposeful, problem-solving play indeed is one of the most important avenues through which children learn (Luckenbill, Subramaniam, & Thompson 2019).

As Jung & Recchia (2013) explain, "Because what motivates infant play is the pure joy of mastering objects and actions, play is viewed not as a means to an end but as an end itself. In play, infants interact with their environment, absorbing new information, solving problems, acquiring actions, and learning to adapt to the world" (829–30).

Nell and Drew (n.d.) write about five essentials of meaningful play:

1. Children make their own decisions.

2. Children are intrinsically motivated.

3. Children become immersed in the moment.

4. Play is spontaneous, not scripted.

5. Play is enjoyable.

The impulse to play comes from a natural desire to understand the world. This play impulse is as strong as a child's desire for food or sleep (Nell & Drew n.d.).

To support infants' and toddlers' learning, follow the children's lead for what they need, as Carolee does:

> Shawna (8 months) pulls a toy piano off a low shelf in her infant room. She pushes one key and a sound emerges. Surprised, Shawna pushes the key again. Smiling, she pushes another key. Shawna's teacher, Carolee, moves in closer to observe. When Shawna looks up at Carolee, the teacher says enthusiastically, "You pushed a key! You made music."

Carolee thoughtfully follows Shawna's lead during play. Carolee places the piano on a low shelf where Shawna can easily see and reach it. The teacher knows that an 8-month-old can easily push a large piano key to make a sound. Carolee observes and sees that Shawna is experimenting with cause and effect. Shawna discovers that she causes the effect—the sounds—and repeats the movement. The teacher does not show her how to do it. Instead, Carolee observes while Shawna explores the toy, and when the time is right—when Shawna invites her into the play by looking at her—Carolee says enthusiastically, "You made music."

Provide Time for Exploration

Play requires time. Play involves children choosing their activities in an enriched environment that you create. In some toddler classrooms, the children stay together all morning and move from activity to activity together as a group. Observe what can happen when young children cannot make choices and do not have uninterrupted time to explore what interests them:

> After the toddlers eat a snack together, the teachers take them all to a puzzle table. Time is limited. Some toddlers want to explore the puzzles longer, but it's time to move to the next station. One child is very distressed at leaving his puzzle unfinished. The teachers move all the toddlers to two water tables, where they have 15 minutes to explore the properties of the water. Some toddlers are tired and out of sorts by this time and start to cry. The teachers tell the toddlers to get their coats and line up to go outside. Some are so eager to go outside that they plow ahead, and the teachers scold them. Finally, everyone is outside and there are just 15 minutes to play before it is time for lunch.

Compare the scenario above with the one below. In which room would you feel your needs would be better met if you were a toddler? In which room would you prefer to be as a teacher?

> Sara, a young toddler, finishes her snack with the other toddlers. The teacher helps her wash her hands and says, "What would you like to play with today? We have blocks and sand and other toys," as she points to each choice.
>
> Sara immediately heads for the blocks. She sees the new sticky blocks and tries to bang two of them together. They stick! Sara was not expecting that. She experiments with the blocks for 15 minutes before going off to find her friend Sam. She pulls on his arm to come to the storybook area where there are low chairs and couches, a rug, and some pillows. The books are displayed so that the children can easily see the covers and choose a favorite book to look at.

Sara first tries a well-established schema or way to handle blocks. She is surprised by the unexpected outcome. This causes her to explore the blocks with great interest; she is learning about the different properties of objects. When she tires of the blocks, she wants her friend to join her in another activity. Because the toddlers in this room are encouraged to make choices about what they will do, Sara has learned that she can invite another child to join her in her play.

In Sara's room the teacher thoughtfully arranges interesting materials, including some that Sara and the other toddlers have not experienced before. These materials spark Sara's interest and challenge her thinking. The teacher gives children the gift of time to explore, quench their curiosity, and learn. The teachers also observe and facilitate children's engaged and enthusiastic learning through play.

Scaffold Children's Learning

Adults play a significant role in helping young children learn and enjoy learning (Bruner 1978), and scaffolding is an important part of this practice. "Scaffolding allows children to solve a problem or carry out a task that is beyond their current abilities. It is a bridge teachers create to connect existing knowledge to new knowledge and understanding" (Gillespie & Greenberg 2017, 90). When you encourage a child's efforts or persistence, expand on her language, give her a hint or suggestion to try, or help her focus (Klein & Feldman 2007), you are scaffolding that child's learning.

In Chapter 6, scaffolding was discussed as a strategy to support young children's cognitive development. However, scaffolding also includes emotional support. Teachers scaffold emotional development and cognitive learning when, for example, they play peekaboo with infants and young toddlers. During this activity, the teacher models and adjusts her movements, words, and facial expressions to engage in a beautifully choreographed, synchronized dance with the children (Jung & Recchia 2013). The adult "stimulates learning through play but also encourages their [infants'] active participation" (Jung & Recchia 2013, 832). When infants initiate a game of peekaboo after many instances of responding to your initiations, you know that you have empowered them to play and learn with you. Caring relationships form as you and the infants share the joy of interacting.

Dance the Developmental Ladder

The term *dance the developmental ladder* describes how teachers notice whether an activity is too easy or difficult for a child and then adjust their strategies to the developmental level of the child (Honig 1982). This is a form of scaffolding. Here are several examples of how one teacher dances the developmental ladder.

> When Antonio's teacher Tammi notices that he had a trying time holding regular crayons, Tammi dances down the developmental ladder. She finds crayons that are easy for Antonio to handle with a hammer grip. Antonio feels successful when using his new crayons. When Tammi observes that Cecelia is becoming bored with 10-piece puzzles, Tammi dances up the developmental ladder and offers puzzles that are more challenging. To help Cecelia with the more challenging activity, Tammi reminds Cecelia about the strategies she used with the easier puzzles. Cecelia uses many of the same techniques to finish the more challenging puzzles.

Each child may be on a unique rung on different ladders of development. Although Cecelia is adept at fine motor tasks like puzzles, Tammi notices that she needs extra support with large motor activities.

Provide Affordances to Support Success

Affordances are creations or adaptations that you make to the environment, for example, to playgrounds, to support success for each individual child (Gibson [1979] 1986; Kleppe 2018). In the following example, Damian creates affordances that provide challenges for the children in his room who are ready to pull themselves to stand and walk around an object.

> Damian, a teacher in an infant room, facilitates the children in his care who are learning to pull to stand. He places a crate that they cannot tip over in the middle of the floor. This is like a piece of furniture in the infants' homes. The children, including Jamal, who has special motor needs, investigate the crate. They soon begin hanging on to the crate and cruising around it.

— — —

> Terek, a toddler, seems driven to run and climb. His teachers notice that his need to be always on the move means that he seldom interacts with the other children or with materials that don't lend themselves to gross motor play. Wanting to support Terek's learning and relationships success, his teachers talk together about how they might provide affordances and also challenge Terek in different ways. They use masking tape to create a trail on the floor that weaves around the edges of the indoor classroom. The teachers place feely boxes—shoeboxes with a hole cut out of the top for a sock to fit through, inviting toddlers to reach in and try to guess what's in the box—along the trail for Terek and his peers to discover. The teachers also encourage several children and Terek to run outside on the playground with balls and scarves.

Play Interactive Learning Games

> Christian, a toddler teacher, sits by a big box with an open top and whispers loudly with a sense of wonder in his voice, "Where's Lucias? I don't know where he went." Several toddlers quickly come over to see what's happening. Just then, Lucias pops his head up out of the box. "Oh, there you are, Lucias. I'm so happy to see you." Lucias smiles and laughs. Lucias disappears again, clearly hoping to continue the game.

Interactive learning games involve teachers' responsive, prompt, and fun interactions with children. The teacher's actions build on the child's initiative. Christian knew that Lucias was waiting for his teacher to look for him. Although both of them knew what would happen during the game, Lucias loved getting a surprised and enthusiastic reaction from Christian.

These games help children learn about cause and effect. When you respond, you build infants' and toddlers' sense of agency—their sense of "can do," confidence, persistence, and problem solving. Games also help teachers and children develop relationships with each other.

Here are some more examples of interactive learning games with very young children:

> An infant makes an unexpected sound; you respond by opening your eyes wide in surprise and making your own vocalizations.

> A toddler jumps up and down; you smile, jump up and down, and chant, "Jump, jump, jump."

> A toddler comes up behind you and tickles your leg; you smile in delight and say, "Jasper, you tickled me."

Both children and teachers enjoy interactive learning games. Adults can appreciate children's competence and enjoy interacting with them, while young children delight in games that empower them with the joy of making things happen.

Be a Keeper of the Spirit of the Child

A "care for the spirit" day is one that cares for the essence of the child—the need for love and attention. The Expanding Quality in Infant Toddler Care Initiative in Colorado (Colorado Office of Early Childhood, n.d.) used the term to describe days when children need more attention. Being able to identify these times helps teachers feel and show more empathy for young children who are having a difficult day and need more loving attention, perhaps because they are not feeling well or did not get enough sleep the night before. If a child is clingy or fussy, ask yourself, "What may have happened that resulted in the child needing more loving attention today?" While you may not know the reason, you can tune in to his need for you to care for his spirit.

Understand that infants and toddlers will have days when they are fussy or tired and need your gentle care for their emotional well-being. Recognize that each child is vulnerable if she is left to cry, if her sense of self-worth is diminished, if she misbehaves to get attention, and if her needs for affection and loving attention are not met. When a toddler clings to you, you can keep her close and say, "This is a care for the spirit day." Be kind, generous, reassuring, and positive.

Caring for the Spirit of the Child

I do not care how you look.
I just care that you look at me.

I do not care whom else you love.
I just care that you love me.

I do not care whom you know.
I just care that you know me.

I want you to know that I have a
vacant feeling
When someone new takes care of me.
She does not hold me quite right.
She does not know that I like to
play peekaboo.
I want you.

I care that you know how to hold me.
I care that you are gentle with me.

I care that I can snuggle safely into you.
I care that you are my safe haven.

I care that you hold me when I cry.
I care that you feed me when
I'm hungry.

I care that you listen to me and
talk with me.
I care that you laugh and sing
songs with me.

I care that you focus on helping
me learn.
I care that you wait to see if I can
solve a problem.
I care that you help me when I need it.
I care that you make me happy and
smile a lot.
I care that my family trusts you.
I care that you care.

—Donna Wittmer

A responsive, relationship-based teacher in infant and toddler center and home programs engages in rewarding interactions with children and families. A responsive, relationship-based teacher knows how to be a reflective practitioner, a collaborator with children to facilitate learning, and a keeper of the spirit of the child.

This chapter supports the following NAEYC Early Learning Programs standards and topics

Program Standard 1: Relationships
1.D Creating a Predictable, Consistent, and Harmonious Classroom
Program Standard 2: Curriculum
2.A Essential Characteristics
Program Standard 3: Teaching
3.C Supervising Children
3.D Using Time, Grouping, and Routines to Achieve Learning Goals
3.E Responding to Children's Interests and Needs
3.F Making Learning Meaningful for All Children
3.G Using Instruction to Deepen Children's Understanding
    and Build Their Skills and Knowledge

Chapter 9

Responsive, Relationship-Based Environments

Responsive relationship-based environments support children's needs for affection, affirmation, positive emotional connections, and learning opportunities. A responsive relationship-based environment

> Supports optimal teacher–child and child–child relationships

> Is attractive, calming, and engaging—for example, contains organized wall displays of the children's artwork and live plants and flowers

> Is age, individually, and culturally appropriate—responsive to children's interests and needs

> Includes carefully designed and defined learning areas in the room

> Includes many opportunities for learning in all domains of development in each area of the room and during routines and transitions

> Creates opportunities for the unexpected

> Provides opportunities to experience and appreciate the outdoors and nature

> Creates a welcoming environment for families

Support Optimal Teacher–Child and Child–Child Relationships

When you walk into a family child care home or an infant or toddler room in a center, do you immediately feel that this is a place where strong, positive relationships can develop? Safe gliders are available to rock young children. Infant and toddler teachers may be sitting on the floor with seats that support their backs, so that they are emotionally and physically available to children. There are spaces with room for a teacher and child to, for example, investigate a mirror together or read story books on the floor or in a comfortable chair or low couch. There are cozy spaces for older infants and toddlers to play peek-a-boo with each other or nestle into an inviting corner for two. There is a low bench for families to gather to observe and interact with their children. As you develop or re-create enriched environments for young children always think about how an environment can facilitate trusting, caring relationships.

Provide Attractive, Engaging, and Calming Learning Environments

Well-organized environments in centers and family child care homes allow space for infants and toddlers to move between learning areas. The walls are not cluttered or overstimulating; the wall colors are calming. Arrange children's artwork on the wall low enough for the children to see it. Put colorful mats on the floor to invite mobile infants and toddlers to develop their motor skills. Ensure that the environment is aesthetically pleasing to teachers, children, and families (Hilman 2012).

Provide homey furnishings such as small, low chairs and couches and safe pillows. Set up the reading area for mobile infants and toddlers so that children may sit comfortably on the floor, with lighting that is soft, not glaring. Child-size furniture invites older infants and toddlers to climb into it to "read" books or to sit at a low table to do puzzles or play with clay.

Have short easels available every day to summon toddlers to try painting with foam pieces, large paintbrushes, and assorted colors of paint, and also provide crayons and paper at a low table. Create other inspiring learning areas in the room to engage mobile infants and toddlers to construct, problem solve, experiment, and rest. Ideas are described in detail later in this chapter.

Use safe wooden storage cupboards and shelves that won't tip over when an older infant or toddler tries to climb on them. Place baskets of toys within children's reach on the shelves, labeled in English and other languages represented in the families of the children in your room.

Consider Age, Individuals, and Culture

Chapter 8 outlined core considerations for developmentally appropriate practice from the perspective of the teacher's role. Here, these same considerations—age, individuals, and cultures—are applied to providing effective environments.

Age Appropriate

Environments change as the children in a room grow older and develop new interests and skills. Infant rooms look different from rooms with toddlers. The environments for multiage groups also look different. Following are some materials children at different ages find interesting and challenging (NAEYC, n.d. b):

> Young infants need items they can safely reach for, hold, suck on, shake, pound, and squeeze; things they listen to; and things to look at, including books. They need floor space to practice their motor skills.

> Older infants and 1-year-olds need toys to develop and use their fine motor skills: materials to create and build with, board and cloth books, and puzzles and pegboards. Provide space and equipment to encourage this age group to use their large muscles.

> Older toddlers enjoy toys and materials for solving problems, such as objects to sort, pegboards, shape sorters, and more complex puzzles. They need picture books with more details than books for younger children. They enjoy familiar items for pretend play, like plastic food, dishes, utensils, dress-up clothes, and things to push.

All these age groups need comfortable spaces to build emotionally supportive relationships with adults and peers.

Individually Appropriate

Each day as you interact with infants and toddlers you will observe their

> Interests

> Enthusiastic focus and passions

> Emerging developmental milestones

> Increasing independence in some activities

> Continuing need for support in some activities

Use this information intentionally to create opportunities for play activities and to individualize the curriculum (Shin & Partyka 2017).

Culturally Appropriate

Provide children with "many opportunities to build an authentic understanding of diversity in culture" in nonstereotypical ways (NAEYC 2018, 30). These might include books, posters, and foods reflecting a variety of cultures, photographs of children's families, exposure to languages spoken by children's families and the community, and music and artwork from diverse cultures.

Define Learning Areas

Notice how Isidora's teacher arranges items in the classroom to help Isidora practice her budding motor skills within the trusting child–teacher relationship:

> Isidora (10 months) looks expectantly at her teacher as she eyes the Fun Tube—an eight-foot-long nylon tube for infants and toddlers to crawl through. The teacher exclaims, "You can crawl through the tube. I'm right here watching you." The teacher observes the infant's careful progress through the tunnel. Emerging on the other side, Isidora breaks out into a smile. She excitedly crawls to her teacher for an emotionally refueling hug.

"Environments act as a third teacher in the room if they are well organized and full of interesting developmentally appropriate materials" (Reggio Emilia, n.d). Defined learning areas help you organize your environment and enable infants and toddlers to use materials, toys, and equipment that are similar in each area.

Young infants benefit from safe spots to observe their more active peers. Provide spaces and surfaces where infants lie on the floor to practice their supervised tummy time, rolling, and pushing up their bodies before beginning to crawl. Place floor mats where two infants can lie side by side on their backs and touch each other. These mats on the floor allow children to look, coo, and smile at each other. Offer learning areas where infants can experiment with cause-and-effect connections—such as safe materials to bat at with their hands and feet. Most of all, infants need spaces where teachers hold them, feed them, and rock them and where they can sleep peacefully in cribs while in sight of teachers.

Do not "containerize" infants (Porter, n.d.). Swings, car seats, entertainment centers, and other restrictive devices can inhibit children's physical development. Unless required by a child's medical condition, enable children to move freely and safely on their own.

Mobile infants and all toddlers need clearly defined areas to explore. "Learning Areas and Materials," on pages 91–93, describes typical learning areas found in rooms for older infants and toddlers as well as equipment, toys, and natural materials that invite children to engage and focus. Notice that you can find many inexpensive materials, such as shoeboxes, swatches

of cloth, clothespins, and safe containers, to add to your environment. Always provide safe, choke-proof toys for infants and older children who are still mouthing toys. Carefully and thoughtfully choose materials that

> Can be used by children of many developmental levels

> Are age and individually appropriate

> Interest one child or many children

> Are challenging to several children

> Invite toddlers to play alongside each other and work together

In each area provide shelves and containers. Mark both with pictures and words. Children will learn to classify materials and learn the meaning of symbols (pictures and words).

Create storage boxes of materials and toys that you can bring out to meet individual children's interests and abilities and to replace mouthed items that must be washed. Periodically change the toys on shelves while keeping favorite toys available.

Choose materials to set out each day and week based on children's individual preferences. Many pieces of equipment, toys, and materials stay the same so that children have a consistent environment where they can find what they need. Offer a quiet resting area, water and sand play, easels, crayons and paper, blocks, and dramatic play materials every day. Offer other materials, such as finger paints and playdough, as a special activity on some days. Brainstorm with your team and plan for individuals and the group to keep learning opportunities both available and engaging.

Learning Areas and Materials

Learning area	Equipment, toys, and materials
Fine motor/ manipulative	› Fine motor toys: Rattles, teething toys, stack and sort toys, nesting baskets, stick clothespins and cans with holes in the lid, lacing beads and boards, pegboards, puzzles, puppets, safe-sized balls and containers › Plastic cups for children to explore size, experiment with spatial relationships, create, and use the muscles in their hands and eyes › Books with pictures of toys and flaps that open and close for small fingers
Large motor/ movement	› Short slides › Mats of assorted sizes and shapes safely stacked at different heights for children to climb › Balls and baskets of assorted sizes › Filmy curtains hung safely so that children see through them and play run and chase or peekaboo › Tall cardboard cutouts that children peek through and run around › Large boxes that children pop out of and climb in and out of, and that have cut-out windows to peek through › Books about crawling, walking, running, and jumping › For older toddlers: A wooden stump, goggles, toy hammers, pegs to pound into the stump
Blocks and construction	› Wooden blocks of all sizes, sticky blocks, wooden people and animals, toy vehicles, wooden train tracks and trains, masking tape for roads, Duplos or similar snap-together blocks › Containers to fill and dump › Books about construction equipment and projects, trains, and vehicles
Creative	› Child-size tables and chairs › Varied sizes and colors of crayons (always available), several types of paper and surfaces on which to color, cardboard, sandpaper, and other interesting surfaces › Playdough and tools: spoons, cups, rolling pins › For toddlers: glue and paper scraps, cotton balls, stickers, yarn, ribbon › For toddlers: easels and paper on short tables, paint, finger paints, different tools to use to paint—sponges, brushes of varied sizes and shapes, and cars with wheels › For older toddlers: Clay and tools

(continues)

Learning area	Equipment, toys, and materials
Sensory experiences	› Waterproof aprons › Water table or small dish tubs for individuals—water table toys, waterwheels, bubbles, sponges, funnels, plastic bottles of assorted sizes to fill, hoses, floating and sinking toys, dolls, washcloths, basters, measuring cups and spoons, nature items such as shells, safe-sized rocks, and wood pieces with safe edges › Contact paper: on the floor to walk on, on the wall to stick things to; feathers and other materials to stick on the contact paper › Sand table with scoops and shovels, cardboard juice cans with holes on the sides so that sand can flow out in interesting ways, funnels, shovels, scoops, containers and materials, plastic dinosaurs › A variety of samples of materials and objects with different textures—soft, rough, silky, shiny—such as sandpaper and fur › Scent boxes › Bubbles to chase and pop
Reading and literacy	› A low bookshelf that displays books in a way that lets children see the covers and reach the books easily › Comfortable sitting areas for teachers and children and nooks for two children to look at a book together › Pillows for toddlers › Basket of homemade books with pictures of the children, families, pets, and so on
Dramatic play	› Household items: small pretend stove, refrigerator, and sink; pots, pans, food, and utensils; toy telephones; small grocery cart › Dress up: clothing that represents the families and cultures of children and several mirrors; uniforms, hats, purses, and a place to hang up clothes › Dolls and clothing from different ethnic groups, pretend baby bottles, blankets, small gliders, doll beds, small strollers and wheelchairs, soft animals › Materials for pretend play with themes familiar to the children: doctor, market, restaurant, and so on
Math and science exploration	› Plants (nonpoisonous) › Fish tank with fish, other pets (compliant with health regulations) › Natural materials such as safe-sized rocks, pine cones, leaves to feel and sort › Safe-sized magnets and magnifying glasses › Light tables and materials › A mirror above the table › Books about plants and animals

Learning area	Equipment, toys, and materials
Cozy corners for adults and children	⟩ Firm, but comfortable, surface and stuffed animals (for toddlers) ⟩ A long safety mirror attached carefully to the wall at children's eye level ⟩ A carefully supervised big box open on one end with pillows and blankets inside for toddlers
Rest and sleep	⟩ Cribs for infants ⟩ Safe mats on the floor for toddlers ⟩ Blankets and security objects from home for toddlers
Outdoors	⟩ Places of shade and rest ⟩ Water tubs or table, water toys (in warm weather) ⟩ Small hills, gardens (if possible) ⟩ Safe movable items such as milk crates, boxes, pieces of wood, tires ⟩ Sand areas that can be covered; containers, shovels, scoops, pails, and water for wetting the sand ⟩ Large paintbrushes and well-supervised small containers of water that toddlers can use to "paint" sidewalks ⟩ Natural materials: rocks, shells, twigs, leaves, pine cones, mud, puddles, stumps; trees and bushes for children to see, touch, and smell if possible ⟩ Playhouses that invite dramatic play and peer social play

Provide Many Opportunities to Learn

Teachers are sometimes concerned if older infants or toddlers want to spend all their time in the fine motor/manipulative center in the room. Do not worry. When you are intentional about providing many types of materials in each area and intentional in the ways you interact with children, they learn in all the domains of development in each learning area and throughout the day. For example, provide opportunities for children to learn and use language and other ways to communicate in each learning area and during routines like diaper changing or toileting. Provide materials and opportunities in all areas to support the following:

⟩ Teacher–child relationships: comfortable low chairs or couches for teachers; handmade books showing teachers and children; strategies to build trust, have fun together, and be responsive to children's needs

⟩ Peer relationships: cozy nooks for two or three children, boxes with holes cut in the sides so that older infants and toddlers can hold each other's hands or peek at each other through the holes, multiples of favorite items, support for prosocial interactions, books about friends

- Emotional experiences: language that helps children understand and express emotions (talking, singing, and reading about emotions), books about emotions and compassionate interactions, materials to help children reenact familiar scenarios and work through feelings (dolls to care for, phones to talk on)

- Language experiences: responsive language interactions; talking about materials, experiences, and feelings; books and photos; objects similar to those found in children's homes

- Thinking: materials and support for curiosity, experimenting, problem solving, mastery motivation, and thinking about others' perspectives

- Motor and movement: opportunities to use both small and large muscles as well as balance

Create Opportunities for the Unexpected

Create opportunities to foster children's curiosity, observational skills, and investigation. Events that cause *disequilibrium*—puzzlement and questioning—spark children's investigations to find out more. Observing the unexpected is one way to do this; it enhances infants' learning and desire to explore (Stahl & Feigenson 2015, 2017).

> Ahmed (15 months) toddles over to the block area, where a container of Duplos catches his eye. He dumps all of the blocks on the floor. He jams two Duplos together and then picks up a strange-looking block. Imagine his surprise when this block doesn't fit together with a Duplo. What is it? Ahmed looks around and finds one other sticky block in the pile. He sticks those two blocks together and looks around for more.

When objects behave in unexpected ways, infants and toddlers pay attention. Ahmed finds himself having to compare the two types of blocks and experiment with their properties (Schulz 2015). He stays focused and experiments with the blocks for a long time.

Appreciate that look of wonder in children's eyes; their curiosity leads to learning and to the love of learning.

Support Respectful Relationships with the Environment

Respectful relationships with the environment develop as children and teachers, over time, explore and deeply appreciate the outdoors and nature. Provide opportunities for children to become attuned to nature and wonder at the beauty and variety of its many facets. Bring the outdoors inside when possible, particularly if your options for spending regular time outside are limited.

The outdoors and nature stimulate children's senses in special ways (Honig 2015). Give children plenty of opportunities to be outside. Infants and toddlers may listen alertly as crows high up in the sky caw back and forth. Older infants and toddlers can sniff fragrant flowers planted in an outdoor garden. They will enjoy with keen attention the flare of red on a robin's breast as the bird tugs in the grass for a tasty worm to eat. With excitement, toddlers may be the first to spy spring bulbs starting to poke through the earth. In warm weather they love to wiggle their bare toes in mud. If you provide a well-supervised shallow wading pool, they will happily feel the cool pleasure of splashing water with their feet.

Exploring the outdoors is crucial for young children's physical and emotional health and well-being (Honig 2015; Hopwood-Stephens 2015). Outdoor play

> Allows opportunities for infants and toddlers to use their large muscles to run, jump, and climb

> Offers time for toddlers to create things with movable items like crates and boards

> Lights the spark of peer play as toddlers run, build, climb, chase, and slide together

Shade is necessary. Comfortable spots for reading and puzzles will encourage children to enjoy a calm activity when they need it. Child-size benches and chairs foster peer jabbering or talk. Make sure there's a comfy area for teachers to use to provide respite for exploring infants and boisterous toddlers, which creates opportunities for caring relationships to develop (Wittmer & Petersen 2018). Having a small playhouse invites social interactions and pretend play.

Invite children to dig for special rocks or wooden animals hidden in sand. As toddlers scoop and fill different-sized containers, they learn about concepts such as full, empty, more, less, half, and whole as teachers use these words to narrate the play and to increase children's vocabulary. Digging in a sandbox lets children feel the grainy texture of sand. Provide pie tins that they can fill with lightly wet sand to make "pies." Give older infants and toddlers big, wet sponges to wash the riding toys and to use to squeeze water into the dirt and sand.

With camera in hand, go on a photo hunt with toddlers and have them tell you what to photograph. Then create a slideshow and ask the children where you took the photo. Some toddlers may be able to use simple cameras. Their photo choices will enlighten your perspective on their view of the world!

Create a Welcoming Environment for Families

What helps you feel comfortable and welcome? How does your program help family members feel welcome?

Provide comfortable places for adults within the children's environment in order to encourage family members to visit. A place for families to sit comfortably for a moment at the end of the day acknowledges their needs and encourages family members to renew their relationship with their child. Provide a secluded area for breastfeeding.

Add photos of the special people in the children's lives to the walls and in small photo books. Families from diverse cultures feel more comfortable and welcome in the environment if there are photos of all the families of the children in that room or family child care home displayed prominently on the wall with a title such as "Our Families." Use posters of diverse cultures and labels in English as well as children's home languages to let families and visitors know that you recognize, respect, and welcome everyone.

Responsive, relationship-based environments provide for both positive emotional connections and wonderful learning opportunities. Defined learning areas help you organize an environment that is age, individually, and culturally appropriate. Teacher–child, family–teacher, and child–child relationships blossom as teachers create environments that spark young children's needs for safety, security, love, and learning.

This chapter supports the following NAEYC Early Learning Programs standards and topics

Program Standard 1: Relationships
1.D Creating a Predictable, Consistent, and Harmonious Classroom
Program Standard 2: Curriculum
2.A Essential Characteristics
Program Standard 3: Teaching
3.A Designing Enriched Learning Environments
3.B Creating Caring Communities for Learning
3.E Responding to Children's Interests and Needs
3.F Making Learning Meaningful for All Children
Program Standard 9: Physical Environment
9.A Indoor and Outdoor Equipment, Materials, and Furnishings
9.B Outdoor Environmental Design

Chapter 10

Routines and Relationships

Routines like greeting, diapering, and feeding are a vital component of the curriculum—what children experience each day. Use these experiences to invite learning in all domains of development—emotional, social, language, cognitive, and motor. Each is an opportunity to build children's sense of self-worth, self-regulation, and emotional well-being, so make the most of each routine to enhance early relationship intimacy and early learning.

Health and safety are paramount. Review your state or local child care rules and regulations for detailed information and rules on how to keep children safe and healthy during all the following routines.

Develop Relationships Through Responsive Routines

Each routine has its rhythm that young children come to depend on. Routines provide children a sense of safety and familiarity with predictable sequences each day. They are opportune times for relationship building and learning.

Welcome New Children and Families

When an infant or toddler is going to start in your program, it's a challenge to focus on supporting the child's and family's emotions and developing your relationship with both the child and family, yet all are important to consider (Bang 2014). Entering an early childhood program for the first time or transitioning to a new program is stressful for young children. Your comforting, reassuring actions can help children become more comfortable and reduce stress (Bernard et al. 2015). Build trust through your loving and intimate focus and cuddling with a child entering a new care situation.

If possible, visit a family's home before they bring the child to your center or child care home. Also encourage families to visit the program with their child and spend time there before leaving the child. Talk with families about their home routines—how the child likes to be held and fed and what her favorite foods are. Ask the family what people, toys, music, animals, and books spark her interests. Talk together about their goals for their child as well as their cultural preferences. Having this information—and continuing to have these conversations with families—will allow you to provide a responsive, individualized care and learning program for each child.

Provide Compassionate Greetings

Separating is hard for most infants and toddlers until they are familiar with the program. Encourage parents to create predictable goodbye routines (Luckenbill, n.d.). Try to greet each family and child warmly. As families say goodbye in the morning, be ready to gently hold an infant or toddler or take a toddler by the hand to show her a familiar or new, enticing activity.

A child may experience renewed separation anxiety if he has experienced any type of family change—a move, a divorce, a new sibling. Encourage toddlers to talk about their feelings around these changes. If a toddler is upset and crying when a parent leaves, you might say, "You feel sad when your daddy leaves. I know you miss your daddy. Daddy will be back after your nap. Do you need a hug?" Offer to walk the child to a fish tank to see the new fish. Say, "I wonder if that new fish is hiding behind a rock? Let's go look," as you take the child's hand.

Use Empathic Diapering

> Luca (15 months) goes over to his teacher, Jenni, and says, "Poop." Jenni responds, "Oh, did you poop?" Luca heads for the diaper table with Jenni close behind. Novah (15 months), on the other hand, protests each time a teacher needs to change her diaper. After Jenni problem solves with her co-teacher, she decides to try a new strategy to help Novah feel more comfortable with diapering. Jenni sits down beside Novah on the floor, and when Novah finishes playing with a toy bus, Jenni says, "Novah, it is time to change your diaper. Do you want to walk, or do you want me to carry you?" Novah exclaims, "No!" Jenni says, "I'll take your hand, and we can jump to the diaper table." As Jenni starts jumping, Novah looks at her and starts trying to lift one foot.

An older infant or toddler may not be ready to pause her activity to have her diaper changed. Be sensitive to this, and notice when a toddler who is busy playing finishes exploring the toys. Then chant, using the child's name, "Time to change your diaper, Miki." Waiting until the child finishes a task shows respect for her activity. If you must change a child quickly, tell her that it is time for a diaper change rather than swooping in to pick her up. Reassure the child that she can return to her activity when you are done.

If a child consistently resists diapering, look at the situation from his perspective. Does he feel safe on the changing table? Is the table comfortable and warm enough for him?

Involve children in the diapering process. Talking about what you are doing while you are doing it is a form of self-talk that comforts children *and* helps them learn language. Infants and toddlers learn language, self-help, and self-regulation skills during diapering with responsive teachers (Laurin & Goble 2018). Think of diapering as the opportunity to engage one-on-one with language and positive emotional interactions with a child.

Diapering often means that there are fewer teachers in the room who are available to the other children. Scout, a 14-month-old who had just started in a program, screeches in an ear-piecing voice whenever her favorite teacher goes to diaper another toddler. The teacher understands and places Scout beside her as she changes the other child.

Each state has its own licensing rules regarding diapering. Post these for all adults to see as they are diapering.

Feeding and Eating: Caring and Communicating

Feeding routines differ for infants and toddlers.

Infants. Infants show hunger in a variety of ways. Some cry loudly; others may whimper or frown. Learn each child's cues and feed infants when they are hungry. Feeding hungry infants as soon as you can meets their physical and emotional needs and develops their trust in your care.

Cradle infants for bottle feedings. Some children suck vigorously on the bottle, while others sip casually as if they were on a beach soaking up the sun. Other curious infants have to stop sucking and look around many times as you feed them. Respect each infant's timetable as well as his individual temperament and style of eating. Some like eye contact, and others will nestle in to you with their eyes closed while holding on to one of your fingers.

Breastfeeding mothers will either express milk so that you have it available in a bottle or take time from work to feed their child. Provide a quiet place with a glider for them to nurture their infants both physically and emotionally.

Toddlers. Eating together at mealtimes creates feelings of togetherness and enjoyment of others (Mortlock 2015). Sit with toddlers as they eat, and encourage animated conversations. These conversations increase toddlers' language development (Degotardi, Torr, & Nguyen 2016). Teachers hovering above children eating does not lead to engaging teacher–child or peer interactions. Respectfully help toddlers gently wipe their mouths with a clean cloth and wash their hands after they eat. As you do so, use descriptive and caring words to support children's self-help skills, language development, and emotional development.

In some programs, minimal teacher–child interaction occurs during observed mealtimes (Hallam et al. 2016). There is little teacher talk, and there are low levels of responses to children. Most of the communications to children are directives, such as "Eat your food." In contrast, mealtimes are important social experiences for children in quality programs. Teachers and toddlers talk about a wide variety of topics, including the food and children's recent experiences (Rhyner et al. 2012). Toddlers sit in low chairs around a circular table so that they engage with each other. Older toddlers may create their own rituals (Mortlock 2015), such as singing as they wait for their food. Appreciate the social bonding that occurs as toddlers laugh together.

Soothing, Sleeping, and Napping

Infants have their own sleeping schedules, and each may need your special way of helping her fall asleep. During their first year of life, place young infants on their backs to sleep (AAP 2016b), which helps to prevent sudden infant death syndrome (SIDS). See your state's child care regulations for detailed health and safety guidance.

After lunch and before naptime, routines such as washing hands and brushing teeth increase toddlers' feelings of comfort because they can predict what happens next. Often, they drowsily move toward their favorite blanket and the comfort object waiting for them on their mat and nestle in. Some toddlers want you to sing or gently pat their backs. Each child clues you in to know what he needs to drift off to sleep. As toddlers waken, greet them warmly and encourage them to move toward a quiet activity if others are still sleeping.

Sensitive Toilet Learning

Teachers who help children learn to use the toilet engage in one of the most private and intimate practices in the profession. Handle this with care. Toddlers *learn* to use the toilet; we do not train them. Toddlers must feel the urge to urinate and have bowel movements. Then they must make it to the toilet in time. They discover over time what each bodily sensation means. They learn to stop playing and often run to the toilet. These skills are hard to learn.

There is a very wide age difference for coordination and mastery for opening and closing urethral sphincter muscles (for urine) and anal sphincters (for bowel movements). Some toddlers sit still on a short toilet by 24 months. Other toddlers are constantly on the move and find it difficult to sit still; learning toileting skills may be harder for them. They may not master the coordination required until they become preschoolers.

Some children are particularly fearful of having a bowel movement. They cannot see what is happening as muscles push a bowel movement out of the back side of the body, and they urgently feel the need to stay safely in diapers. Respect the different timetables toddlers may have in mastering the muscular coordination needed for toilet learning. Shaming or coercing only makes children feel more fearful and more determined not to learn. This may lead to emotional as well as physical difficulties concerned with toileting activities. Patience, perceptive attention to children's differences, gentle coaching, and acceptance of each child's timetable support this process.

Toilet learning is a joint cooperative endeavor with families. Together with families, go over the prerequisites for toilet learning, including learning words for pee (urinate) and poop (bowel movement), feeling the need to use the toilet, and being able to sit still for quite a while on a child-sized toilet. When a family understands these prerequisites, you and the family are more likely to decide together in a cooperative way on a toilet learning timetable. Family and program differences require open communication and information about toddler physical and emotional readiness. Consistency at home and in the program is of utmost importance to a child's success.

Do not be concerned if toddlers touch their own genitals. They are curious about body parts and how they work. This is typical behavior and if ignored, will likely stop. Provide the names for body parts and describe in simple terms how they work.

Pickup Time

By day's end, many children seem to wilt. They lose some of the zestful energy in play they have shown during the day. Some toddlers need sensitive teachers to carry them in their reassuring arms, even though they walk quite well. Some children may run to the back of the room or outdoor play area when a family member comes at pickup time. To ease the transition, encourage the parent to talk with the toddler about what the parent and child will see or do on the way home.

Try to say goodbye to each child and family member. If your program uses something like a Summary of the Day form, share it with the family. If possible, describe something special that their child learned or did that day, such as "Aarav tasted broccoli today," or "Candace and Matthew imitated each other trying to jump today."

Create a Thoughtful Schedule of the Day

Schedules make the program day predictable and reassuring for young children. Keep in mind that schedules of the day are guidelines, not set in stone. Being responsive to individual children's needs requires you to be flexible.

Infants

Young infants set their own schedules. They nap when they need to sleep and eat when they are hungry. Infants feel safe when they can predict that their favorite teachers will take care of them, talk with them in reassuring tones, feed them when they are hungry, help them to sleep when they are tired, and be there to greet them when they wake.

Toddlers

Toddlers feel secure when they generally can predict when they will have snack, play in the room, have lunch, nap, go outside, and go home. The sequence of activities is more important than the actual time allowed for each. The group may seem to need more playtime on a given day. With a sudden storm, toddlers may not be able to go outside as usual to play and they may act cranky and upset. Offer simple, calming explanations to help toddlers become aware of the need for altering plans when necessary. Have them look out the window at the pouring rain and hail and talk about what will happen they go outside. They will all get soaking wet and shivery! This tool of asking "What will happen if . . ." stimulates toddler thinking skills and helps them reflect on times when change and flexibility become necessary.

While long group times are not appropriate for toddlers, if you say, for example, "I have a book about bears to read to you!" in an enthusiastic voice, toddlers will often come running. Others may be busily playing and not want to gather together right then. Respect their choices. During play, always initiate reading books or singing songs with individual children and respond as they show interest in these activities. Invite small groups of children together to share with them something special, such as a beautiful flower or caterpillar crawling outdoors.

A typical schedule for a toddler or multiage room is shown on page 103. Know that many children will need a snack and definitely a drink before going outdoors. Always, these are not rigid times. On a day when many toddlers are intensely engaged in a project—such as playing with boxes—morning indoor playtime may be longer. Remember that during playtime, your role is crucial: be emotionally available, intentionally observe what children are learning, and use strategies to support them.

Sample Schedule for Toddler or Multiage Group	
Morning individualized greetings, breakfast (in many programs) and child choice/teacher responsive playtime	7:30–9:00 a.m.
Snack and greeting songs	9:00–9:30
Indoor playtime—Child choice/teacher responsive playtime Songs and stories with interested individuals and small groups of children during playtime	9:30–10:30
Outdoor playtime	10:30–11:30
Lunch time	11:30 a.m.–12:30 p.m.
Nap time	12:30–2:30
Individual children waking and playing	2:30–3:00
Snack time	3:00
Indoor or outdoor child choice/teacher responsive playtime	3:30 until child goes home
Goodbye time: sing a goodbye song to each child or use another reassuring ritual	Before child goes home

Guide Transitions Throughout the Day

Transitions are times when you and the children change what you are doing. These points are often challenging for everyone, causing stress and turmoil unless you help children predict what will happen next. When toddlers are engaged in their play, they often do not want to change activities and go to the table to eat or go outdoors. When toddlers are outside, they often do not want to come inside again. Cleanup time for toddlers is especially challenging. Following are some ideas to make transition times easier for everyone:

> Understand that your goal is to help each child feel safe.

> Try to reduce the number of transitions for children by providing extended periods of time to play, eat, or go outdoors so that they do not feel hurried.

> Be as consistent as possible with the schedule. Children feel more comfortable when they know what happens in sequence each day. When routines are the same each day, toddlers learn that after they pick up toys, they go to the door and then outside with a teacher.

> When playtime is almost over, give toddlers verbal and nonverbal clues (hold up a photo, sing a song, play a sound). Make up a song you consistently use to indicate this transition, like "It's cleanup time, it's cleanup time. Time to put our toys away."

> Talk about what will happen during and after transitions. Say, "We are going to put away our toys now, and then we will go outside."

> During cleanup time, give clear directions in a pleasant tone of voice and offer positive feedback, for example, "Tomas, here is the blue block. Put the block on the shelf with the other blocks. Thank you. You did that so fast! You put the blue block on the first shelf."

> Label shelves and containers with pictures and words to make cleanup easier for children.

> When it is time to eat or go outside, chant the same chant each day. Create your own, such as "Now it is time to eat our food, eat our food, eat our food. Now is the time to eat our food, on this beautiful day with you."

> When it is time to come indoors, create a ritual like marching in rhythm, chanting, trying to walk quietly like a mouse, or holding hands.

> Sing songs and do fingerplays if children are waiting, for example, for lunch.

Routines and transitions are times for your kind, considerate, and respectful responsive behaviors. When you are emotionally available to meet children's needs and scaffold learning during these times, you support children's development in all domains of learning.

This chapter supports the following NAEYC Early Learning Programs standards and topics

Program Standard 1: Relationships
1.D Creating a Predictable, Consistent, and Harmonious Classroom

Program Standard 2: Curriculum
2.A Essential Characteristics
2.K Health and Safety

Program Standard 3: Teaching
3.B Creating Caring Communities for Learning
3.D Using Time, Grouping, and Routines to Achieve Learning Goals

Chapter 11

Creating Responsive Learning Opportunities

Curriculum for infants and toddlers is everything that children experience and learn from both planned and unplanned experiences (Wittmer & Petersen 2018). Adults are responsible for creating opportunities to learn:

> In a responsive, relationship-based curriculum, the moment-to-moment, day-to-day, and weekly needs and interests of the children and their families guide teachers' planning process. The infant-toddler teacher does not start planning the curriculum with a list of activities, but rather starts planning for the day or week by observing what the children are doing and learning in all developmental domains. (Wittmer & Petersen 2018, 319)

Infants and toddlers thrive with a rich variety of options and *time* to explore them. There are opportunities for the following:

> Positive and relationship-building emotional connections with caring adults

> Play with peers in an environment that enhances the possibility for budding friendships

> Focused play with materials and toys that are age, individually, and culturally appropriate

> Engagement with carefully designed indoor and outdoor environments that provide rich possibilities for learning and affirmative relationships

> Interactions with teachers and peers who scaffold children's learning

Following a clear, yet rich path will allow you to provide these opportunities for responsive learning. These steps will take you there:

> Observe and document children's relationships and learning

> Use observation to plan a curriculum that is responsive to children's goals, interests, joys, and needs

> Recognize the potential in each activity, toy, and piece of equipment

> Find resources for activities, materials, and environments

> Reflect to understand how your curriculum is working

Observe and Document Children's Interests and Learning

Observing children is key to facilitating their development, learning, and relationships. This process is about "listening to children with care and attention" (Gandini & Goldhaber 2001). It begins with a teacher's interest in noticing each child's development, learning, and interests. Astute teachers also want to know how the group is developing and learning as a caring community.

There are several relationship-based ways to observe, record, and share infants' and toddlers' interests, development, and strategies for learning and then use this information for individualized, responsive planning. These methods of observation encourage teachers to "make learning visible" (Rinaldi 1994). When you do this, families, teachers, children, and team members can appreciate the remarkable intentions and development of each child.

You make learning visible by showing what children know and what they're able to do. Here are some ways to do this:

> Take written notes and photos of children working.

> Collect samples of artwork to share with the children, other teachers, and families.

> Write stories about children's learning (see the story form on page 107)

> Create displays and documentation panels.

> Develop portfolios.

Write Stories About Children's Learning

Stories share what a child is doing and learning in your program. Create your own learning stories with space for families to add their observations and photos, too (MOE 2004). An example of a story form to record learning stories is shown on page 107. Use the information on these forms to plan next steps for the child. With parents' permission, post the stories on a bulletin board. Then put them in the child's portfolio to document the child's interests and development.

Create Displays and Documentation Panels

At the beginning of each year, or when a new child enters your program, ask each parent to sign a form that gives permission for you to take photos and post them on walls and in hallways as you create displays and documentation panels.

Displays include arrangements of photos, examples of children's work (for example, the scribbles of an older infant), and information for families. Arrange them on walls and bulletin boards, placing some low enough so that infants and toddlers see them easily. Laminate pictures and Velcro them to a wall, so that young children can pull them down and carry them around.

Observation Story Form

Child:	Date:	Teacher:

Observation and Responsive Planning

Today Daniel enjoyed lying on his back and looking at a book. He concentrated on his book for about 5 minutes. He turned the pages and focused on each page. He seemed to feel calm and safe as he played with the book. Once in a while he looked at his teacher as if to share his discoveries. His teacher said in an admiring voice, "Daniel, you are looking at a book."

What is the child learning?	Responsive planning
Daniel is using his eyes and hands together to manipulate the book. He demonstrates his ability to attend and focus. He is problem solving how to turn the pages. Daniel's receptive language is growing as he listens to the teacher's words.	We will provide more books for Daniel to play with when he is lying on his back. When he turns over, we will place a book in front of him to explore in a different way. We will ask his family what books he is enjoying at home. We will provide more fine motor activities because he seems to enjoy using his hands and eyes together.

Ideas from home

Following are some ideas for displays that promote enjoyment and learning for children, family members, and teachers:

> Photos of infants and toddlers playing and working hard at achieving their goals, for example, a young infant shaking a rattle, raising hands for "so big" games, hammering a peg board, or sitting and pointing at pictures while jabbering to herself with a beloved picture book

> Samples of children's artwork, such as the paint lines of a toddler, with a title, "I am learning to use the fine muscles in my hands—I am learning to create"

> A photo of each child as a newborn beside a photo of each child now with the title, "See how I have grown"

> Pamphlets, brochures, and other information for families

> A written and picture schedule of a typical day

> Information on the week's special events

Use these displays as a way to help children revisit their learning. For example, talk about what they did as they look at a sequence of photos of their block building, their absorption in bathing a doll, or their poring over a picture book with a peer huddled close.

Documentation panels highlight examples of children's interests and learning (Seitz 2008). Panels often include a sequence of photos and focus teachers', families', and children's attention on the process of what and how children learn. See an example of a documentation panel on page 109.

Observations for documentation panels often begin with teachers' and family members' probing questions of interest. Questions like these are inspiring and focus adults' attention:

> How do infants or toddlers communicate with each other, including their facial expressions and gestures?

> What do infants or toddlers learn when they play?

> How do toddlers play with blocks? What are they learning?

> How do children use the small muscles in their hands?

> How do young children show caring, comforting, and kindness?

> What songs and chants are children learning and participating in with gestures and body movements?

> How do toddlers focus on an activity that interests them?

> How well do toddlers show that they act flexibly when desires cannot be met immediately?

You and your coteachers, in collaboration with families, will think of many more questions to spark your inquiry about children's interests, development, and learning. Creating documentation panels will give you ideas about further ways to enrich the environment and learning experiences for the children.

Documentation panel. Marcus seems to know where the top of the toy is even though he can't see it (A).

He turns the top of the large box toward himself and takes out one of the smaller boxes and places it on the floor. He reaches in to try to take out another box (B).

Marcus is curious and engaged. He investigates how the boxes fit inside each other (C). Marcus is learning about how objects take up space. At 11 months of age, Marcus is a competent learner when given opportunity and time to explore interesting toys and materials.

Develop Portfolios

One method of collecting information is to develop a portfolio for each child. You may decide to create a digital portfolio that families can access. A three-ring binder works well, too. Start with the name, the age, and a photo of the child on the front cover. If you start the portfolio at the beginning of the year and continue adding to it throughout the year, you will create a special document that captures the wonderful growth of each child. Always date each entry. You might include the following:

> Photos of children's development milestones (from teachers or family), such as when an infant uses a pincer grasp for the first time to pick up food items.

> Photos of sequences of children's actions (see the documentation panel on page 109). Write below the photos what the toddlers said and did and what they were learning. If several children are in a photo, make a copy for each child's portfolio.

> Photos or notes that illuminate how children learn, such as a toddler trying to put objects in a big plastic container with a small opening. Highlight the fact that the child uses many different strategies to accomplish his goal.

> Photos or notes that capture children's emotional, social, language, thinking, and movement development and learning.

> Children's artwork.

Involve Families in Observation and Documentation

Families are an important part of observing and documenting children's interests, learning strategies, development in all domains, strengths, and needs. Add photos from the family to the child's portfolio, and soon it becomes a program and family *collaboration collection* of valuable information. Make the portfolios available for families to look at throughout the year and take home at the end of the year.

Encourage families to give you feedback on your displays and documentation panels. You deepen parent participation, and you also get more ideas to help you plan learning opportunities.

Use Early Learning Guidelines

In order to observe and plan effectively, of course you need to know typical child development progressions. This knowledge affirms your observation skills and will bring joy to your work. As you look more closely, you will begin to note subtle beginnings and small steps in development. For example, you'll appreciate when young infants bring their hands fully together in the middle of their bodies. This means that soon they will bang items together to learn more about objects, and they will learn how to play pat-a-cake. Share your enthusiasm about new developments with co-teachers and families.

To learn about sequences in children's development, use your state's early learning guidelines that profile development from birth to age 3. See *North Carolina Foundations for Early Learning and Development* and Head Start Early Learning Outcomes Framework as examples. These include developmental sequences in approaches to learning and in social, emotional, language, cognitive, and motor development. Many early learning guidelines also include suggested activities for each domain and age group. Compare your state's information to several other states for context and a broad understanding.

Many programs use assessment tools, such as the HELP Strands 0–3 and The OUNCE Scale, to document children's development. Your program could use these along with early learning guidelines to learn about developmental sequences, document each child's growth, and plan opportunities for each child in your group.

As important as early learning guidelines are, they do not capture young children's interests, goals, strategies, strengths, and needs. Observation often tells us more about children's capabilities and how to plan. For example, assessment tools usually do not consider individual differences in how long children take to master different skills. The normal timeline can be short—a "narrow window" (Honig 2014)—as it is for using their thumb and finger to pick up objects (pincer prehension). Or the timeline can be long—a "wide window"—such as for learning to walk steadily, talk clearly, or master toilet learning.

However, observation, documentation, early learning guidelines, and assessment tools used together help you follow children's lead for what they need.

Use Observation to Plan a Responsive Curriculum

You can use your observations of children and your knowledge of child development to plan appropriate and engaging interactions and environments for individual children and the group.

Planning involves preparing, arranging, changing, and adapting interactions, activities, and the environment to promote an individual child's and the group's love of relating and learning. Planning should be responsive to children's ages, unique interests, and cultures. For example, an infant may have difficulty with some fine motor skills. Based on your observations and discussion with the child's family, you adapt your interactions with this infant to support his use of his fingers, hands, and eyes. You might place colorful rattles near the infant's hand to encourage him to pick them up and shake them. Or you may observe a toddler who tries to hold a paintbrush but drops it. You then provide *experiences* for her to strengthen the muscles in her hands and fingers. Both cases demonstrate responsive, individualized planning.

Plan for Relationship-Building

Planning in a relationship-based way always includes using children's interests to build adult–child and peer relationships. For the child who loves puzzles, create an enticing puzzle area with a table against a wall and two chairs. For those fascinated by water play, provide enough funnels, cups, strainers, and spoons for each child using the water table. Or, better yet, for toddlers, provide four tubs of water, creating a square from the tubs. Children have their own tub and materials while watching and talking with their peers. One day add dolls that toddlers can wash and dry with sponges and cloths. Provide blankets so children can wrap dolls up tightly to keep them warm; shoeboxes lined with dish towels make comfortable beds for dolls. Provide more than one of the same toy. One bucket in a large sand area does not lend itself to peer relationship building, and it invites conflict. Five small buckets with scoops and one large bucket invite multiple children to cooperate to fill the large bucket.

Plan by Observing Individual Children's Goals, Interests, and Experiences

Each day or week, observe and record the interests and intentions of each child. Notice what children are learning and think about what you might plan that will expand on it. For example, an older infant may have an interest in exploring where objects go when out of sight. To expand on the child's interest in learning about object permanence, provide more small cloths to hide toys under or containers where toys disappear but are easily found and retrieved.

We call this *responsive day-to-day planning*. Notice what attracts individual children's interest and contributes to their focused attention and excitement about learning. If mirrors suddenly catch an infant's or toddler's attention, then provide a few more in the environment and determine to spend more time one-on-one with that child exploring mirrors. If a toddler is really enjoying watching construction equipment that is busily paving a street near the program, add construction trucks to the block area and make roads out of masking tape on the floor.

Build on children's experiences with their family. Does a child have a new brother or sister? Provide the toddler with dolls and soft animals, cradles or doll beds, bottles, small high chairs, blankets, small tubs and sponges to wash dolls, and child-size gliders. Did a family recently visit a zoo? Add wooden zoo animals and cardboard boxes to create homes for the animals in the manipulative area. Provide picture books of animals to read together.

You become a responsive program planner extraordinaire when you observe what sparks individual children's interests and then provide materials and experiences that build on what motivates their learning.

Plan for the Group's Goals and Interests

Responsive planning also builds on a common interest of the infants or toddlers in your group. If many infants are shaking toys, you may want to create a shaking toys project. You can take photos of the varied styles that children use to shake objects. If the young infants prefer certain toys to shake, then make sure there are more of these. Look for materials that make different sounds, and wonder with the children about the differences. Provide varied materials for the infant to shake a toy against, which may lead to children banging objects. Your shaking project could result in a documentation panel that explains what children are doing and how they listen as they shake different objects on the varied materials. Parents and other teachers will be excited to learn how these young infants experiment with sound and cause-and-effect relationships. Demonstrate with documentation how infants develop a sense of competence as they experiment with "making things happen."

Perhaps you see that your toddler group is fascinated by water—where it comes from and where it goes. Consider creating a water project. "Planning for Children's Interest in Water," on page 113, has several ideas for materials you might choose to add to your existing environment, along with activities to explore with the children based on their interests.

Planning for Children's Interests in Water	
Learning area	**Equipment, toys, and materials**
Fine motor/ manipulative	Find soft, squishy fish filled with water to manipulate. Provide an opportunity for interested toddlers to pour water in and out of different sized containers. Help them observe how the same amount of water fills one container but not another.
Large motor/ movement	If possible, find a Fill n' Fun Water Mat for infants to crawl or walk on. Sing "Row, Row, Row Your Boat" in small informal groups. Pretend to row a boat as you sing. Move like fish through pretend water.
Blocks and construction	Blocks and construction toys should always be available.
Creative	Provide big, wet sponges for children to use outside to "paint" the sidewalk or boxes. Talk with toddlers about what they see happening.
Sensory experiences	Add play fish to the water table with scoops or slotted spoons and buckets or strainers. Provide small nets to catch the fish. Add items that sink and items that float, small waterwheels, flexible tubing, and containers of different sizes.
Reading and literacy	Find toddler books on water to add to the reading corner. Read books to informal groups of children. Possibilities: > *Where's the Narwhal?*, by Ingela P. Arrhenius > *Llama Llama Learns to Swim* based on the series by Anna Dewdney
Dramatic play	Provide water in bottles to feed dolls that drink. Provide individual tubs of water to wash dolls. Add soap, small washcloths, small towels, and blankets.
Exploration math and science	Freeze water in small containers and then watch the ice thaw in the water table. Find plastic tubing so that the toddlers pour water into one end of the tube and watch it come out the other end.
Cozy corners	Provide soft stuffed fish and fish puppets.
Outdoors	Provide small containers of water to add to the sand table. Talk about how the sand changes when water is added.
Songs	Sing "The Water Song" to infants and toddlers (https://www.youtube.com/watch?v=tquUKGCaFZs). Find the *Pinkfong Baby Shark Official Sound Book* by Pinkfong.
Special events (e.g., walks, visitors)	Ask families if they have ideas for where you could walk with your group to see a fish tank in your neighborhood.
Families	Ask families what questions their toddlers may have about water. Ask what toddlers like to do with water at home.

Ask toddlers, "What do you like to do with water?" They might say, "Drink," "Splash," or "Make bubbles." Document their answers with photos and display them where families, other teachers, and especially the children can review their thinking. Toddlers can choose among the possibilities for learning that you offer. In addition to water, interests could include topics such as friends, emotions, spatial relationships, curiosity, and many other areas. For infants, topics could include spatial relationships, object permanence, cause and effect, and opposite concepts such as "up and down" or "open and close." Always follow children's lead for expanding on their interests and the strategies they are using to learn, such as shaking toys, putting objects into and taking them out of containers, and experimenting with the concept of cause and effect. You will not have all of the materials for this project; however, you can collect materials gradually. Perhaps you can share with another teacher. You will find a blank form for planning for children's interests in the appendix.

Note: *Always monitor children's use of water carefully. Children have drowned in a few inches of water. This topic is primarily for toddlers.*

In Chapter 12, we provide another way to plan, using storybooks that are interesting to the children in your group as the centerpiece. For example, you may observe that the toddlers in your group are expressing emotions, and they are still learning about how to interpret others' emotional expressions. You could find storybooks and songs about different emotions and then add other materials to learning areas that support the focus on toddler emotions.

Recognize the Potential in Each Activity, Action, Toy, and Piece of Equipment

> Lulu (4 months) lies on her back on a firm mat on the floor. She gazes up at her teacher, Sam, and smiles, trying to engage Sam to pay attention to her. Sam leans toward her and in a kind voice says, "Hi, Lulu. You look so happy." Lulu smiles back and makes soft cooing sounds. Sam follows her lead and makes soft cooing sounds back to Lulu, then picks up a rattle and shakes it gently in front of Lulu's hands. She reaches out and grasps the rattle.

In this simple interaction, Lulu learns so much. She feels effective at gaining Sam's attention. She gains trust in the kindness of her special teacher. She hears the sounds he makes and processes which ones are more likely to follow others. She engages in a cooing conversation. She sees the rattle and reaches out to successfully grasp it, wrapping her fingers around the handle. She gazes at the rattle and then shakes it. When shaking the rattle makes a sound, she shakes it again. She gains confidence in her ability to "make things happen."

Embedded in each experience is the potential for infants and toddlers to learn. In the following example, what do you think Rebecca is learning?

> Rebecca (11 months) sits by a group of kitchen utensils hanging from a bar on a sturdy structure. She grabs a spoon and bats at the utensils. They clang together. Delighted, Rebecca continues batting at the utensils, creating a symphony of different sounds. Felicia (10 months) crawls over to see who is making the noises. Rebecca moves over and makes room for Felicia to sit by her.

There is so much learning happening, it is difficult to describe it all. Rebecca is learning about spatial and cause-and-effect relationships. She is developing a "can do" attitude. She is practicing her social skills by engaging positively with Felicia, and she is enjoying the sounds she's making. She is an active learner. Look for the potential in each activity.

Find Resources for Activities, Materials, and Environments

Many activity books for teachers have ideas to try with the infants and toddlers in your care and learning program. As you read about these activities, decide whether the children in your care will (1) enjoy them and (2) learn from them. For example, would at least several of the toddlers in your room enjoy trying to toss different-sized balls into a basket that you place in the large motor/movement area? Why do you think that? What adaptations will you need to make to the activity to meet the interests, strengths, and needs of your group? Some children may be ready to handle smaller balls, while others will need bigger ones. Still others will like textured balls. Your wise judgment as to which activities to make available and how to adapt them will determine how beneficial they will be.

Reflect to Understand How Your Curriculum Is Working

As you move through the days using your responsive, relationship-based curriculum, set aside time to reflect with your co-teacher on your continuing observations. Here are some ways that you know your curriculum is working:

> All infants and toddlers are comfortable spending time with you. You are often at their level, so they approach you, sit on your lap, hand you toys, or nuzzle next to you.

> Young (nonmobile) infants are with and beside you. You are holding them or they are lying safely on the floor near you. They may be practicing their movements. They may be engaged with you in a "serve and return" interactive game of cooing and smiling. They are *never* placed in car seats or other devices that restrict their mobility unless they have a disability that requires a special device.

There's No Time for Screen Time in Infant and Toddler Programs

Infants and toddlers need your responsive interactions and interesting environments to become enthusiastic learners. A study of over 2,400 children in Canada found that toddlers have an average of 17 hours of screen time (from television, video games, computers, tablets, and smartphones) a week. More screen time for toddlers predicted lower developmental scores at age 3 (Madigan et al. 2019). Video chatting is considered positive screen time, however, because the child participates in responsive social interactions (Kirkorian, Choi, & Pempek 2016). The American Academy of Pediatrics (AAP 2016a) recommends no screens for infants and toddlers younger than 18 months, limited high-quality programs for children 18–24 months watched with an adult, and only one hour a day for children 2 and older. Share information about screens with families. They will need to decide when, where, and why they want and may need their infants and toddlers to experience screen time at home.

> Older infants and toddlers are engaged with you, peers, and materials in the environment. There are also signals that they are happily involved and learning. Children demonstrate

- Concentration: Children's attention is directed toward the activity

- Energy: Children have energy to focus and be exuberant at times

- Facial expressions: Children often have an intense look or are listening carefully; they also often smile

- Persistence: Children do not become easily distracted; they show determination to examine or use materials and toys

- Satisfaction: Children seem happy, content, and proud of their accomplishments, such as wrapping a doll in a blanket or tossing soft balls into containers

> Children are experiencing a sense of well-being, excitement, low stress levels, happiness, and loving relationships.

> Children are developing and learning.

> Families feel respected and happily engage with you often.

Teachers plan for relationship building, children's goals and interests, and the group's interests. Follow each child's lead for what he or she needs and what captures his or her interests and focused attention. Each experience provides the potential for learning in all domains of development.

This chapter supports the following NAEYC Early Learning Programs standards and topics

Program Standard 1: Relationships
1.D Creating a Predictable, Consistent, and Harmonious Classroom
Program Standard 2: Curriculum
2.A Essential Characteristics
2.J Creative Expression and Appreciation for the Arts
Program Standard 3: Teaching
3.A Designing Enriched Learning Environments
3.B Creating Caring Communities for Learning
3.D Using Time, Grouping, and Routines to Achieve Learning Goals
3.E Responding to Children's Interests and Needs
3.F Making Learning Meaningful for All Children
3.G Using Instruction to Deepen Children's Understanding and Build Their Skills and Knowledge
Program Standard 4: Assessment of Child Progress
4.B Using Appropriate Assessment Methods
4.C Identifying Children's Interests and Needs and Describing Children's Progress
4.D Adapting Curriculum, Individualizing Teaching, and Informing Program Development

Chapter 12

More Curriculum Ideas: Singing, Music, and Reading

Nurturing a deep love of books and music in the first three years is so important that this entire chapter is dedicated to ideas for singing, listening to and making music, and enjoying books with children.

Sing to and with Children

Caring teacher–child and peer relationships develop as you sing with infants and toddlers. Singing with little ones often brings smiles to their faces as you sing to one child on your knee or several children close to you.

Toddlers proudly and happily sing familiar songs during play, often oblivious to anyone else. They can easily learn their names and their peers' names when they are used in songs. They often beam when you use their name in a song, and then point to another child when they hear that friend's name. When they sing new songs at home, they can engage family members who may feel proud of the child's memory and ability. Most important, songs let the singers express pleasure, and they build bonds between teachers and children and peers (Fink & Marxer, n.d.).

Sing with and to children during many times of the day. Singing builds many skills as well as contributes to children's love of music.

> Social-emotional skills develop as children share and take turns, cooperate with peers, sing about emotions, and practice self-regulation skills, such as waiting for a new song to begin. Singing contributes to infants' and toddlers' positive emotional experiences and connections.

> Language skills develop as children learn unfamiliar words (vocabulary). They learn the sequence of language (syntax) and, importantly, enjoy listening and using language in a new way. They learn about rhythms and rhymes, which are essential aspects of early literacy and lead to later reading skills.

> Literacy skills also develop as infants and toddlers see pictures, photos, and words that teachers show them as they sing.

> Children learn about each other's families and cultures when the group sings songs from different home cultures. If you know them, sing songs in other languages. Ask family members to come into the program and sing with the infants and toddlers.

> Children learn thinking skills such as counting, patterns, and sequences and develop their memory. They learn about symbols as they use spider puppets when they sing "The Itsy-Bitsy Spider" and you show them a picture of a spider weaving a beautiful web on garden bushes, and they also gain the vocabulary word *spider*.

Singing songs during transitions helps children learn to predict and enjoy the transitions, including waking up, cleaning up, going outdoors, and goodbye times.

Infants and toddlers relax with certain types of songs, enjoying the melodies and comforting rhythms. Lullabies are especially powerful for soothing fussy infants (Honig 2005).

Change the words of songs for a child or group, such as including details about them or things they like. Create new chants and songs. For example, you could chant, "Molly is here, hi Molly; Omari is here, hi Omari."

Infants and toddlers do not care if you feel you cannot sing very well. They will enjoy you *and* your voice. They like the feeling of community and belonging as they sing together.

Listen to Music and Introduce Musical Instruments

Listening to and making music nurtures children and supports learning. Parlakian & Lerner (2016) recommend the following ideas to support children's love of listening to music:

> Hold infants and sway gently to music.

> Help infants and toddlers move their bodies to music. Introduce different tempos and observe to see if infants change their movements.

> Introduce music from a variety of cultures.

There are many wonderful CDs of children's songs. Raffi's *The Singable Songs Collection* box set will motivate children (and you) to sing along and move to the music.

Create a box of musical instruments with duplicates so that older infants and toddlers can experiment with how to make sounds. You can make musical instruments using ideas from Red Tricycle: www.redtri.com/homemade-instruments/slide/1. The page explains in detail how to make rain sticks, sensory bin shakers, xylophones, singing straws, paper plate tambourines, and cereal box guitars. You can also provide pots and pans for children to play using a safe, large spoon. Here are some more ideas for how to provide and use musical instruments:

> Organize different instruments in baskets for infants and toddlers to explore.

> Place a basket of instruments in front of two infants sitting together. They will explore and imitate each other.

- Give each child in a small group an instrument to shake or play while listening to or singing a favorite song.

- Let children bang on toy drums or wave bracelets of bells on their wrists.

- Create a musical parade with each toddler using a different instrument.

- Encourage one toddler to play a musical instrument while other children dance with scarves.

- As children explore musical instruments, use words such as *loud*, *soft*, *fast*, *slow*, *high*, and *low*. Use the correct names for instruments.

Most of all, have fun as infants and toddlers sing, listen to music, and experiment with musical instruments.

Read to and with Children

Early literacy skills refer to the skills that lead to reading and writing. Toddlers begin to recognize stop signs and other familiar symbols in their environment. They begin to scribble on paper and use paintbrushes to paint. Some older toddlers like to try to write some letters in their names. Model how to write their names after you ask them for permission to write their names on their artwork.

Infants and toddlers learn to love reading because you read to them. Give them many opportunities to look at books while turning the pages to enjoy the pictures. Reading to and with infants and toddlers is one of the most important activities you do with them to prepare them for a life of learning and academic success. "Shared book-reading that begins soon after birth may translate into higher language and vocabulary skills before elementary school" (AAP 2017).

An infant nestled into an adult's lap gazes at the bright colors on a page in a cloth book. He listens to the rhythm of the words. He sees a picture of a baby and hears his favorite adult declare, "Oh, baby. You are a baby. See the blue hat on the baby's head," as the adult points to the hat.

— — —

Two toddlers snuggle in closer to their teacher as she sits on the floor with them. They see the pictures in the book she holds and hear her voice. As soon as they see a picture of a cat, one yells, "Kitty!" The teacher says, "Yes, you have a kitty at home, don't you? What does your kitty say?" The toddlers both declare proudly, "Meow, meow."

Both teachers in these examples involve the children in their book reading, engaging their attention and making the experience an interactive conversation. Pause for infants and toddlers to participate while reading picture books. When you share a story with children, encourage them to actively engage with it. When you talk about the pictures and stories, and children relate them to their own experiences, a book comes alive.

Talking with children about a character's emotions encourages children's love of reading as well as prosocial attitudes. When you ask open-ended questions, such as "Why do you think the little mouse is so afraid?" "How do you think the baby deer feels when sees his friend, the turtle?" or "What do you think Daddy will do next?" toddlers learn to solve problems and use language to explain. This type of reading, called *dialogic reading* (Folsom 2017; Whitehurst et al. 1988), leads to children's increased vocabulary and early reading skills.

While reading, hold infants on your lap. Older infants and toddlers may want to lean against your legs as you sit on the floor. Read to toddlers in *small* groups so each one easily sees the pictures in the book. Talk about the subject of their gaze—you don't want them to hear the word *giraffe* if they are looking at a turtle. Be responsive. Some older infants will point at the distinct pictures in a book made especially for them. Some toddlers can sit long enough for you to read two pages. Other toddlers who are comfortably snuggling with you can stay for a much longer book sharing time. Engage infants and toddlers with your voice tones and excitement about the content as you read.

Place books in their own special, comfortable area away from the large motor area, as well as in all the other learning areas in the room. Then toddlers will pick them up and bring them to you to read.

If you do not have a big budget for books, you can make books with pictures from magazines. Laminate them or slip them in plastic sleeves to protect them, and tie yarn through holes in the sides of the pages to make a book. Talk with infants about what each person or animal is doing. Encourage toddlers to tell you a story about the pictures. Add a word or two to the bottom of each page to introduce toddlers to letters and words.

You may want to borrow books from the public library. These, however, will be books that you read to children, rather than letting them explore with their hands and mouths.

Observers in infant and toddler child care programs found that only 1 in 13 infants from 4 to 8 months experienced teachers reading to them during the day. Only half of infants 9 to 12 months heard a book read each day (Honig & Shin 2001). We hope that with increased knowledge of the importance of reading to infants and toddlers, you will read to them every day and even many times during the day.

Use Storybooks to Plan for Individual Children and the Group

In Chapter 11, you learned about ways to plan for individuals and groups. Another way to plan is around children's storybooks (McCord 2011). Start with a book or books that you know might attract an infant's or toddler's interest or that might speak to a stage of development or need, such as a need to learn how to help others.

> Charlie's mother tells his teacher, Jasmine, that she took Charlie (27 months) to the zoo over the weekend. She says that he was excited when he saw a baby giraffe and baby pigs and ducks. Because of Charlie's new interest, Jasmine chooses a book about baby animals for the infant and toddler multiage room this week. She reads the book many times to an infant sitting in her lap. She invites toddlers to come and sit by her on a short couch as she reads the book to small informal groups. She lets families know about the special book that she's reading and recommends it in a short newsletter to families. She adds interesting real and pretend items to each learning area.

Based on the book or books you read, plan on using many levels of representation. HighScope, an early childhood curriculum approach (see www.highscope.org), recommends providing materials and experiences at many levels of representation, from concrete to abstract. The following plan gives examples of levels of representation based on Jasmine following Charlie's interest in baby animals.

> Real experiences:

- Discover the baby animals that children may have at home or that they have seen.

- Provide visiting baby animals.

> Symbolic experiences:

- Provide posters or photos of baby animals.

- Display pictures of the children's animals. Cover them with clear contact paper on cardboard so children can carry them around.

- Sensory table: add small, safe, plastic or wooden animals for the children to discover in the water table or sand table.

- Creative experiences: provide cookie cutters shaped like baby animals for toddlers to use to paint and with playdough.

- Group time or dramatic play: encourage children to use their bodies to pretend that they are baby animals—hopping like a bunny or galloping like a pony.

- Manipulative/small motor area: offer puppets, puzzles depicting baby animals.

- Large motor area: create a trail in the room with masking tape and hide stuffed animals along the trail.

- Informal group times: sing songs about baby animals and use props.

- Reading corner and books around the room: read stories about baby animals and let children explore sturdy books about animals.

› Highest level of symbolic understanding:

- Print the names of the animals beside the posters or photos.

- Display the names of the children on a low bulletin board with a picture of the child and/or the child's family and any pets they have or baby animals they have seen recently.

You can plan the same way using books about birds, flowers, spatial relationships, and prosocial behavior.

Think about the concepts that children learn from a book and provide opportunities in the environment to explore those concepts. For example, think about how the children in your room understand and express emotions, and create posters of the children expressing different emotions. Add more books on emotions to the reading area. Find songs to sing about feelings, and try making different emotion faces with toddlers. Add dolls that express different moods to the dramatic play area.

Multiple opportunities to explore a variety of materials that represent a particular topic help infants and toddlers learn. They need real experiences: seeing, touching, smelling, hearing, and tasting. Also ensure that you expose children to a variety of levels of symbolic understanding, including pictures and words.

Engage Older Infants and Toddlers in Small Informal Group Times

Toddlers love short, active group times. You do not need to get them ready for preschool by making them sit for extended periods. Some will be able to be still and enjoy a story with a small group, while others need to move. The key ingredient to successful small group times is making sure they are engaging.

Small, informal groups allow children to see the print and pictures in a book. Entice toddlers by announcing that you will be reading a book in the reading corner, for example, and that each child will hold a puppet. Toddlers often come running at such an invitation. As you read the book, involve children by inviting them to participate in telling the story by holding up and moving their puppets. Encourage small groups of children to participate further in reading the book by making statements or asking questions.

Stories with flannel boards usually keep children's interest. For example, each toddler could have a flannel piece for the book *Brown Bear, Brown Bear, What Do You See?* (by Eric Carle). As you read the story, each child places his piece on the flannel board. After the pieces such as brown bear, red bird, purple cat, and blue horse, you might tell the story again without the book. Wait after each question to see if the toddlers answer whom the animal sees next.

Alphabet Whizzes?

Feeling the pressure for their children to achieve academic success, some families want their toddlers to learn the names of the letters in the alphabet and even learn to read. Reassure families that while learning to read and write does indeed start with infants and toddlers, you are facilitating their literacy development when you

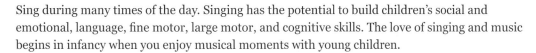

> Develop children's feelings of security through loving relationships that allow them to feel safe enough to focus enthusiastically on learning

> Nurture children's love of books and reading by reading to them often

> Name the letters and words in books when children point to them

> Support children's use of the fine motor muscles in their hands and eyes to scribble, color, and paint

> Support listening skills as children sing and listen to music and listen to storybooks read aloud

Share with families how you are boosting early literacy. If possible, share a list of books that you frequently read to the children in your group. Ask family members for the names of the children's favorite books that they enjoy at home.

Sing during many times of the day. Singing has the potential to build children's social and emotional, language, fine motor, large motor, and cognitive skills. The love of singing and music begins in infancy when you enjoy musical moments with young children.

Infants' and toddlers' early literacy interest and skills grow tremendously during the first three years with literacy-responsive teachers and families. Rejoice at the boost for early literacy that you are providing!

This chapter supports the following NAEYC Early Learning Programs standards and topics

Program Standard 1: Relationships
1.D Creating a Predictable, Consistent, and Harmonious Classroom
Program Standard 2: Curriculum
2.A Essential Characteristics
2.D Early Literacy Program

Standard 3: Teaching
3.A. Designing Enriched Learning Environments
3.B Creating Caring Communities for Learning
3.E Responding to Children's Interests and Needs
3.F Making Learning Meaningful for All Children

Chapter 13

Adult Positive Guidance and Children's Relationship Challenges

Being with infants and toddlers offers many opportunities to use positive guidance strategies that demonstrate your empathy toward children and move them forward in their development. The following are common examples in infant and toddler programs:

Tomo (8 months) crawls over to Peter and pulls his hair, which is shining in the light from the window.

Lila (18 months) exuberantly grabs her friend Suki around the neck, and they both tumble to the ground.

Freddie (20 months) bites Colton on the arm when he reaches in front of Freddie to take his toy.

Keiko (2 years) throws herself on the floor and cries when he has to wait for his teacher to get ready to go outside.

In this chapter, we provide many examples of how to help infants and toddlers manage their strong feelings and learn to be kind and helpful to others. These ideas help children learn how to be healthy, happy, creative, and productive members of their community. This first starts with us as adults being kind and helpful to children and modeling thoughtful behavior.

There is a real contrast between positive guidance and power assertion (Kim & Kochanska 2015). Guidance involves teaching, modeling, and supporting positive behavior. Adults need to be warmhearted and kindhearted with children and sensitive and responsive to infants' and toddlers' needs and challenges. Positive guidance results in infants and toddlers feeling secure and loved, not resentful and angry.

When adults use power assertion techniques, they act critical and negative with children. They may, for example, force a toddler to go to time-out. They may yell at a child, "Sit down, now," or they may say no without providing a reason or without demonstrating empathy for a young child's difficulty waiting or wanting something he cannot have. An adult may withdraw love or threaten to leave until a child complies with the adult's wishes. And adults may try to over-control young children. For example, one teacher we observed wanted the toddlers in a group to sit still without moving a muscle for two minutes before they could eat. Of course, this led to many tears as the food sat in front of them and they tried not to wiggle. Power assertion techniques often lead to young children's anger, defiance, sadness, and unwillingness to cooperate. Or there can be compliance when the adults are present and sneaky noncompliance when the children are unobserved.

Instead of using power assertion techniques, use positive guidance strategies that work. As you come to know each infant's and toddler's temperament and strengths, you will choose strategies that work with *individuals*. Your strategies will change as children mature since they develop skills to express their feelings and needs, understand more reasons, and are able to think about how others feel.

Use Guidance Strategies

This section provides a list of 20 positive guidance strategies. You probably use many of them already. Some may feel new to you and will require frequent practice so that you become comfortable using them. These strategies focus on adults and children building strong, caring relationships with each other. When challenges such as pushing, hitting, and biting occur, positive guidance strategies focus on relationship rebuilding and restoration with both adults and peers. The long-term goals for children are the ability to do the following:

> Enjoy and engage in healthy, caring relationships with adults and peers

> Develop a strong and positive sense of self

> Develop self-regulation skills

> Understand and express emotions in healthy ways

> Become prosocial: take the perspective of others, feel empathy for other's fears and troubles, be helpful

> Problem solve: come to agreeable solutions to resolve conflicts

Ask yourself whether the strategies you are using accomplish these goals.

You want infants and toddlers to internalize ways to treat themselves, others, and their environment. Then they will not need others to control them. With your help, toddlers will be on their way toward self-regulation with you as a co-regulator. Use one of more of the following 10 strategies to prevent challenging behaviors and help children learn emotional and social skills.

1 **Know child development milestones so that you have reasonable expectations.** There is often a disconnect between what adults believe infants and toddlers can do to control their behavior and the realistic developmental abilities of children. This is called the *expectation gap* (Zero to Three, n.d.). This gap leads to adults' *and* children's frustration and stress.

2 **Support children's secure attachment to you.** Secure attachments free infants' and toddlers' emotional energy for loving and learning. Your sensitive, kind responsiveness helps them develop a secure attachment to you and models empathy. Your kindness also models prosocial behavior for children to imitate.

3 **Be emotionally warm and kind.** Warmth is an adult characteristic that meets infants' and toddlers' great need for affection, builds a sense of self-worth, and predicts a young child's ability to manage strong emotions and behavior (Moran, Turiano, & Gentzler 2018). Warmth includes affection, as well as heartfelt and sincere concern for children's well-being. It is the opposite of rejection, aloofness, and unloving voice tones. Infants and toddlers know when you genuinely enjoy them and love being with them.

4 **See and say the positive.** Use encouragement, not praise. Encouragement uses specific words with an admiring tone of voice. Praise includes comments such as "Good girl," "Good job," and "That is great!" Often, infants and toddlers are not sure what you are referring to when you use praise. Encouragement, on the other hand, inspires children to continue the behavior and teaches them vocabulary and concepts. When an infant pats another peer *gently*, say, "Kate, you are patting Liliana so gently. Look at Liliana's face. She is smiling. Liliana likes that." When you comment on a positive behavior, you are both affirming the kind child's behavior *and* helping children take the perspective of another.

5 **Use emotion talk and empathy as well as perspective-taking strategies.** Show compassion and empathy for young children's emotional displays with your face and body. Really listen to infants and toddlers. Read their emotions and comfort them, while helping them learn to express and manage difficult emotions. Help children read each other's emotions; aid toddlers in taking the perspective of other children.

6 **Be a co-regulator with infants and toddlers.** Be the copilot who helps calm children when they become distressed: hold and rock an upset child, and model how to think through problems rather than come apart emotionally. If a toddler drops to the floor and falls apart emotionally (a tantrum), use empathy statements and say, "I know you are feeling sad (angry, frustrated). You really wish you could have the whole box of crayons, but Vir needs some, too. I will help you choose your favorite color."

7 **Assume and see the good intentions.** A toddler who wraps his arms around another toddler may cause them both to tumble down, and you may just see them fall. Assume good intentions.

8 **Use specific words of thanks and encouragement.** Notice if an infant touches another child gently or a toddler helps another child. Acknowledge this by saying, "You helped Sammy. You moved over on the bench so he could sit next to you. He really liked that. He loves sitting next to you. Thank you for helping."

9 **Set safe boundaries with consistent, frequent messages.** Use statements like these: "I will keep you safe," "We are kind to our friends," "We help each other," "We keep our friends safe," "We keep our toys safe," "We pat gently," and "We walk quietly through the hall."

10 **Create predictable but flexible routines for infants and toddlers.** Infants feel at their core the protective arms of tenderness when their special people are attentive to their needs. Predictable routines allow toddlers to feel more peaceful and certain about the flow of the day.

Use one or more of the following 10 strategies in the moment—for example, if an infant or toddler hurts another child, conflicts occur, a child has a tantrum, or a child is doing something that is not safe (such as standing on a chair or running fast through the room).

1 **Use empathy comments.** Think empathy first! Say, "You wish you could . . ." or "You really want to . . ." Using empathy comments is one of the most powerful strategies. You might tell an infant who is crying, "I know you are sooo hungry. I'm fixing your bottle right now." Support children's empathy with each other. If a child hits another child, comment on the feelings of the child who hit *and* the victim of the hit. Young children's development of empathy is crucial for present and future successful social and emotional interactions with others.

2 **Use problem-solving strategies during conflicts.** Toddlers engage in conflicts. Try not to intervene immediately unless one child is hurting another. Observe to see if the toddlers work out a solution. However, if a child is hurting someone, you will need to intervene. Even if you saw Thomas hit Kennard, you do not know what occurred prior to the hit. A problem-solving approach is best. Lean down so the children can hear you easily. Use words that are developmentally appropriate. You can say, "I see you are both feeling upset. I see you are having a problem. Tell me what you want." If the children cannot tell you, then state the problem as you saw it: "You both want the truck." This models what toddlers can say to each other in the future. Next you can ask, "What can we do? Do you have any ideas?" When you first start using this strategy, toddlers generally do not know what this means. If they have no ideas for solutions, then give them choices. "You have two choices. Do you want to take turns? I can set the timer. Then we will know when it is time for Matthew (or Thomas) to have a turn. Or, do you want to push the truck together? One solution is to take turns. Another solution is to play together." Counting with your fingers may help toddlers understand they have choices. Hold up one finger as you describe the first option and the second finger as you describe the second option. Another solution to offer, depending on the children's interests, is bringing out another truck for one child to use. Always provide solutions that build positive relationships.

3   **Help children learn positive, alternative behavior.** Say to an infant tugging on another infant's shirt, "Touch gently, like this" (showing how). If one toddler, Alejandro, grabs a toy from Margo, say, "Margo feels sad." Help Alejandro learn words to use instead of grabbing the toy. Alejandro will learn to say, "Me want dat, pease?" ("I want that, please?") If a child hits when she is angry, teach her alternatives—use words, stomp, count to two, find a teacher, hug a stuffed bear.

4   **Give reasons.** Use simple reasons. Say, "It is not safe to stand on a chair. I want to keep you safe. Let's jump, jump, jump down" and hold the child's hands. Or, "We need to walk down the hall." And then in a low voice say, "If we run, we may fall. Thank you for walking slowly."

5   **Give choices.** Choice questions help toddlers make decisions. For example, if a toddler falls apart because she doesn't want to come in after playing outside, you could say, "You are feeling so sad and mad that we have to go inside. You wish you could keep playing outside. Let's hop like a bunny together to the door. A snack is waiting for us inside." If that doesn't work then provide two choices: "Would you like to walk in tiny steps like a little mouse or take big giant steps as we go inside?"

6   **Give clear guidance and consistent messages.** Use simple words that guide a child's behavior. For example, "Please sit down when you eat. I want you to be safe."

7   **Help children take the perspective of others.** If a toddler is crying, ask another toddler, "What would make Kayla feel better? Do you think she would like a doll or a car to hold?" Toddlers often are surprisingly astute at figuring out what would comfort another child.

8   **Use "after/then."** If a toddler does not want to help pick up blocks after playing with them, use "after/then" statements: "After we pick up the blocks, then we will go outside. Here is one block to put on the top shelf."

9   **Use a voice tone that is quieter than the ones that the children are using. Engage at eye level with a child.** If a toddler starts screaming, crouch down to the child's level and talk quietly. Use active listening skills by saying, "You really wanted the doll that Serena has. I can tell you are feeling very [angry, sad, disappointed]. I see a doll in a cradle. Let's go get her."

10   **Use time-in, not time-out.** If a toddler hurts or bites another toddler, what does she learn if you separate her in a time-out? Instead of time-out, help children learn what to do with their often deeply felt emotions. Give toddlers the words to use to tell you or others how they feel. Encourage them to say, "I'm frustrated" or "I feel angry." Tell them that if they need to be alone, they can go to a cozy corner that is created for that purpose. Encourage children to come to you if they are feeling frustrated, angry, or sad. Tell them that you will help them when they feel this way. If a child continues to bite others and you have used the techniques discussed in "Children Who Act Out and Hurt Others: Biting, Hitting, Kicking" on page 130, use time-in *with you* to help a child who bites learn what to do instead. Keep the child with you so that you can support the child's positive social behavior with encouraging feedback and clear guidance.

Make a poster of prevention and guidance strategies and place it in a prominent place in the room or family child care home. Make a mental list of how many you use. As you read about new effective guidance strategies, add them to the list. As you review each one, think about whether it

> Builds infants' and toddlers' sense of self-worth and self-regulation

> Helps them take the perspective of others

> Supports children's enjoyable, healthy relationships with each other

Understand Emotional and Behavioral Challenges

Infants and toddlers often feel challenged. A young infant feels her tummy hurting. She is hungry and wants food, now! An older toddler wants her bib off, now! A toddler wants that magnificent toy that another toddler is waving in the air, now! The toy in the hands of another looks much more exciting than the same toy sitting quietly on the floor. One toddler seems unhappy. His furrowed brow tells you that he is feeling fearful. Another toddler tries to run around the room continuously and has a challenging time focusing on a task for more than a minute.

There are two types of behavior that challenge both children themselves and their teachers. Some children seem unhappy, anxious, fearful, and withdrawn much of the time. Other children have more temper tantrums and use physical actions that hurt other children. Both types of behavior lead to infants' and toddlers' experiencing challenges with both social *and* learning success.

Children Who Withdraw and Feel Fearful

Some children feel reserved, shy, and withdrawn. That is partly temperament. Some children react more strongly to both positive and negative experiences. Scary experiences or harsh parenting practices may contribute to these children avoiding others or hesitating to try new activities.

Gentle encouragement helps children who are hesitant to try an unfamiliar activity (Kiel, Premo, & Buss 2016). Stay with a toddler who is wary about trying a low, safe slide. Hold her hand as she bravely climbs several steps, sits down, and then slides down. For this toddler, letting go and sliding down may feel like falling down the Grand Canyon would to us. Break a task into smaller steps so that the child feels a sense of accomplishment. Research shows that not forcing and not being overprotective helps these children. Make sure to give yourself an emotional pat on the back for your patience.

However, some children who withdraw are socially fearful. They look anxious. They avoid other children. Any negative experience with peers may cause high stress levels. These children need your best efforts to help them feel safe with other children. Provide opportunities for the child who is fearful to do an activity, such as play with water or playdough, with you and with a caring peer.

Children Who Act Out and Hurt Others: Biting, Hitting, Kicking

When one child hurts another, we often feel upset. Our job is to protect the children in our care. We are worried about the child who hurts others *and* the one who is hurt. We want the hurtful behavior to stop!

Ask Questions and Observe

Start by thinking about the child as part of a family as well as the community of a center or family child care home. The child's family may have information on why they think the child is hitting, biting, pinching, or kicking. Is there a new baby? Has there been a separation or divorce? Is a family member often gone from the home? These are times of family transformation that often upset a young child.

Has the toddler now fully arrived at the new development stage of wanting autonomy—making his own decisions? With their hands on their hips, toddlers often rejoice at saying, "No!" to grown-ups loudly, frequently, and happily. This can upset the family and group dynamics! Toddlers are trying to master their muscular coordination and adapt their wishes to the rules and conditions of the adult world. At the same time, they are trying to establish themselves as separate beings with wills of their own. And sometimes they still just want to be a baby. They want you to hold and cuddle them.

Toddlers may react with anger and frustration when they want to make their own decisions and they cannot, perhaps because of safety or skill issues. Think of how you can give toddlers control in other situations that are safe. Let them pound on playdough, choose milk or juice to drink, and choose what book to read. Toddlers need to experience autonomy with connectedness to others. "Autonomy-connectedness is the capacity for being on one's own as well as for satisfactorily engaging in . . . relationships" (Bekker et al. 2008, 746). Toddlers do not want to feel alone. They need adults to understand their need for autonomy while at the same time helping them feel safe within loving relationships.

If infants and toddlers have not experienced compassionate care at home because of family challenges, it may be difficult for them to develop concern for others (Rhee et al. 2013). These children need *your* compassionate care to begin to care about others. Families may need support from community agencies to feel less stressed and be less punitive with their children.

If a toddler did not receive nourishing care in a previous room, center, or family child care home, then the child may not trust adults and may feel a need to protect herself. Be patient, and give her encouraging, loving attention.

Stay Calm

Many adults find hurtful behavior more challenging than shy, withdrawn behavior. While fear and withdrawal behaviors elicit more protective feelings from adults, children's anger and aggression may elicit more anger. If parents or teachers become negative, the cycle of negativity continues (Ryan & Ollendick 2018). If adults become hurtful, intimidating, angry, and frustrated, they are modeling poor regulation skills. If adults react to a toddler's typical negative emotions of anger and frustration with their own anger and frustration, toddlers are more likely to have difficulty with managing challenging emotions at age 3 (Engle & McElwain 2011). Constantly model self-regulation, showing children how you manage your own negative emotions. It is challenging to stay unruffled after witnessing a toddler biting another child. However, it is important for adults to stay calm and give clear messages to children in a composed, serious voice about being kind to each other.

Respond to Biting

If a child bites another child, one teacher will need to attend to the child who received the bite. Firmly tell the child who bit, "You bit Charlie. It hurt Charlie when you bit him. He's crying." Give the child alternatives to biting: "When you are angry [frustrated, want a toy], you can stomp [take deep breaths, like this], and come to me [ask Charlie for the toy]. I will help you. Let's practice stomping [breathing, asking, etc.]." Think of an alternative that fits with the situation. You may need to practice alternatives with the child who bit at a later, calmer time: "Now, what can we do to help Charlie feel better?" For many more ideas for how to handle toddlers biting others, please see Wittmer and Clauson (2018).

To prevent biting and other hurtful behaviors, use the 20 prevention and guidance strategies starting on page 126. Also choose a safe teething toy that you can attach to the child's clothing for the child to bite. Encourage the child to bite on the teething toy frequently.

It is not good to label a child as "a biter." Doing so says that biting is a part of the child's character. Instead, she is a child who "bit another person." It's also important to find ways to admire and use positive comments with these children. A teacher we know greeted a child at the door who frequently tried to hurt others, read a prosocial story to just this child, gave hugs if the child wanted them, stayed with the child continuously throughout the day, emphasized what the child *could do*, helped the child use sign language or words to get needs met, and strived to meet the child's emotional needs. This focused strategy seems challenging. After several weeks, however, the teacher found that the child seemed to feel safe, had learned new social strategies, and did not need such constant attention.

Follow your program's policies for handling biting. Families need to know the policies and know that there are strategies to prevent biting. If a bite breaks the skin, your program handbook should include a rule that you call the family so that they can take the child to a doctor.

When a Child Feels Very Challenged

All infants and toddlers feel emotionally and socially challenged at times. These developmental challenges need to be met with the 20 guidance strategies. However, when a child's behavior interferes with the child's relationships, either adult–child or child–child connections, conduct more in-depth observation. Work with families and the other teachers to figure out the function or goal of the child's behavior. Observation of *when*, *with whom*, and *where* the behavior, such as hitting, occurs helps you begin to figure *why* it may be occurring. Observation will tell you if the behavior occurs because, for example,

> The child is ill or hungry

> There is conflict with one or two of the same children each time

> The child is feeling crowded

> The child feels tense, angry, or anxious

There are many more reasons for challenging behavior among toddlers and twos. Observe the child's energy level, ability to focus, and developmental struggles. Look especially at the child's hearing and language development. Does the child have the language to express himself rather than hit other children? Always think first about a child's health, and second about the child's need for responsive and sensitive care. Does he need more positive adult–child interactions? Is he feeling safe? Is he feeling securely attached to at least one adult in the program?

After observing and making informed guesses about why the child is behaving a certain way, talk with families and develop an intervention plan using positive guidance strategies. As you talk with families, use a problem-solving approach.

Use a Problem-Solving Approach and Partner with Families

A problem-solving approach often works well when talking with families and with teammates in your program. This approach does, however, require time for observation and problem-solving discussions. For example, if a toddler named Maria is quick to hit other toddlers, brainstorm with other teachers and the family. Try these steps:

> First, state the problem in clear terms. Do not use general terms or label a child, such as saying, "Maria is aggressive." Rather, state the behavior: "Maria hits other children when they move in too close to her."

> Look for the reason behind Maria's hitting. *Behavior has meaning*. The behavior meets a need for Maria. Now that you have started the observation process, you will want to share the results with the family. Explore with the family why they think a child may be feeling challenged. Talk with them to see if there have been any changes in Maria's life that may contribute to her change in behavior. Ask them to follow up on any medical concerns they or you have.

> Brainstorm with the family concerning potential solutions for both teachers and family members to try. Together you can decide on a solution or solutions to try that support the child feeling safe and learning new positive behaviors.

> Try a solution. Emphasize with the team, including the family, that with a problem-solving approach, there will be strategies that will not work at first—or ever. If that occurs, evaluate why the strategy did not work and try another solution.

If Families Use Physical Punishment

In February 2019, the American Psychological Association (APA) released a resolution that calls for adults to use alternatives to physical discipline with children. The APA states: "The research on the adverse outcomes associated with physical discipline indicates that any perceived short-term benefits of physical discipline do not outweigh the detriments of this form of discipline. . . . Rather, using physical discipline predicts increases in children's behavior problems, even after controlling for race, gender and family socioeconomic status" (APA 2019). The APA resolution recommends that adults use more positive strategies that teach children how to become productive members of their community.

Include a guidance and discipline policy in your program handbook, and share this information with families when they enter their child in the program. The policy should include statements indicating that "physical punishment, psychological abuse, and coercion" are never used by staff when disciplining a child, although "appropriate use of restraint for safety reasons is permissible" (NAEYC 2018, 17).

Despite the clearly troubling findings on physical discipline, because of learned customs some families use physical punishment as a prominent discipline method. Staff will need to decide carefully how to approach parents in constructive ways to discuss positive discipline tools to use with infants and toddlers (Honig 2020). Some parents may not be aware of how conflicted toddlers feel. Toddlers usually want to have more and more power to do things on their own. Yet they still need adult help and nurturing cuddles. Toddlers want to "be big," but often have difficulties and frustrations with toilet learning, unclear speech, messy eating, and spilled drinks.

Share information with families concerning toddler development. This may help them navigate this stage with more insights and tolerance. Share a variety of your gentle strategies that help toddlers ease into compliance. Explore these possibilities during conversations with family members. During these talks, be sure to ask families how they get their little ones to smile or laugh or giggle, and appreciate the tips that families give you about their successes in positive interactions.

If Infants and Toddlers Feel Severely Challenged, Help Them Now!

A number of infants and toddlers experience social and emotional challenges that interfere greatly with their ability to enjoy warm and caring relationships with adults and peers. Infants and toddlers tell you through their bodies and words whether they are feeling well or distressed. You, the program, and families will need support from community agencies such as the early intervention system for children with special needs and an infant mental health agency if you see behaviors similar to the following:

> A 6-month-old doesn't smile or displays anger or irritability much of the time

> A 9-month-old lashes out at peers when they come close

> A 12-month-old avoids adults and peers

> An 18-month-old bites or hurts other children frequently, even after many attempts to teach the child positive behaviors

> A 24-month-old seems fearful of adults

> A 30-month-old is terrified when a stranger enters the room

Children's early social, emotional, and behavioral challenges predict later challenges if the child and family do not receive early intervention support. It is critically important to attempt to find additional support for children in their early years. Infants and toddlers and their families cannot wait until preschool if the children are feeling severely challenged now.

Children Who Experience Abuse and Other Traumas

Infants and toddlers are particularly vulnerable to child abuse, such as abusive head trauma, which includes what was previously known as shaken baby syndrome as well as other types of head trauma (AAP 2009). Infant and toddler teachers are mandatory reporters. Check your state's website for their department of human services child welfare office for more information about signs of abuse and laws pertaining to reporting. Add information to your program's program handbook concerning the extreme dangers of abusive head trauma and why and how infant and toddler professionals are required to report suspected child abuse to state officials.

We know more now than even a few years ago about the long-term negative effects of abuse and trauma on infants and toddlers, which can last into adulthood (Raby et al. 2018). Abuse and other traumatic experiences decrease children's

> Feelings of well-being, effectiveness, and self-worth

> Trust in adults

> Brain development

> Emotional and social skills

> Academic competence (Raby et al. 2018)

Abuse and traumatic experiences also affect children's physical health (Child Welfare Information Gateway 2019). Young children may experience delayed motor development and more physical illness and obesity (Petersen, Joseph, & Feit 2014). Adults who were abused in childhood experience many more health problems than those who were not abused (Afifi et al. 2016).

Infants and toddlers who have experienced neglect and abuse need your patience and gentle interactions. Some children will cling to you. Others will avoid you. Develop trust by being continually emotionally available and responsive. Remember to give yourself positive recognition for your kindness through the children's long journey toward healing.

Some infants and toddlers experience traumatic events. These events, such as hurricanes, floods, homelessness, or being threatened or hurt, cause children to feel fearful and unsafe. Infants need your sensitive responsiveness. Toddlers will need you to recognize when they feel stressed and confused. Yeary (2018) provides the following example of responsive calm when a toddler teacher had to take toddlers to a safe basement when there were tornado warnings:

> Respond with understanding and compassion to children's questions: "I know this is different; we are going to the basement because the weather siren says we should move to a place that is safe when there are big winds," "We are going to stay here, nice and safe, until the big winds pass," and "I know it is really dark. The storm made the lights go out. But we are safe together here. I can give you a big hug if you would like." (85)

If you are in doubt as to how to handle a traumatic event such as a storm, try to take the children's perspectives and provide the sense of safety and comfort that they need. Discuss possible future traumatic events with other teachers and a mental health specialist to create a plan for how to respond to events that may occur while the child is at the center or family child care home and also ones that may occur in the community.

Positive guidance is different from power assertion. Children who feel challenged emotionally and socially may withdraw and seem fearful or they may act out and hurt others. Use a problem-solving approach with your team and children's families to determine solutions that may work for individual children. Children who experience abuse or trauma need protection and strategies that help them feel safe and build positive, healthy relationships.

This chapter supports the following NAEYC Early Learning Programs standards and topics

Program Standard 1: Relationships
1.D Creating a Predictable, Consistent, and Harmonious Classroom
1.E Addressing Challenging Behaviors
1.F Promoting Self-Regulation
Program Standard 3: Teaching
3.A Designing Enriched Learning Environments
3.B Creating Caring Communities for Learning
3.C Supervising Children
3.D Using Time, Grouping, and Routines to Achieve Learning Goals
Program Standard 8: Community Relationships
8.A Linking with the Community
8.B Accessing Community Resources

PART 4

You as a Professional

We end the book with what it means to be a relationship-based professional in a relationship-based profession. It is both a challenge and a joy to embrace protection, affection, and learning connections with infants and toddlers as necessary components of this work. An infant and toddler professional integrates both loving and learning in their practice with children because that is what infants and toddlers need to thrive.

Chapter 14
A Relationship-Based Profession

Infant and toddler teachers and child care providers are professionals who belong to a critically important profession. NAEYC (2019) has identified the necessary knowledge and actions of early childhood teachers. Infant and toddler professionals

> Identify as professionals in the early childhood field

> Have a code of ethics and engage in ethical practice

> Have an extensive knowledge base and know that very young children's learning and loving go together

> Are continually learning and improving their practice

> Are involved in advocating for and improving the quality of the profession

> Continually engage in self-reflection on their own and their community's biases and work to appreciate cultural, age, gender, and other types of diversity

Working with infants and toddlers is one of the most challenging professions. It is physically and emotionally intense. As a professional, you require vast, deep, and subtle knowledge of child development and program planning.

Despite these challenges, infant and toddler teachers experience joy when with children. The following quotes from infant and toddler teachers describe what keeps them in the profession:

> "My greatest joy is seeing infants and toddlers develop and grow. At our center we do continuity of care, so we get to stay with a group of infants when they move up to the toddler room."

> "My greatest joy is seeing them succeed at anything. I have seen them struggle and finally get the magnets to stand without help."

> "I get great joy when children are compassionate and empathetic. For example, 1½-year-old Thomas squatted down and gently patted a beetle bug that crossed his path in the sandbox. Two-year-old Leslie earnestly tried to assist her little friend who became frustrated when the firefighter hat wouldn't stay on his head."

Power to the Profession

Infant and toddler professionals are part of a movement to improve quality in early childhood programs. Power to the Profession is a national collaboration of early childhood programs and funding foundations focused on "advancing and advocating for an equitable, diverse, and effective early childhood education profession" (NAEYC 2019). The movement addresses career pathways, knowledge needed by early childhood professionals, standards for programs and education and training for teachers, and professional compensation.

Helping Others Understand the Importance of Your Work

Individuals in the community may not understand the importance of your profession. Perhaps you have heard comments like this:

> Cici teaches infants. She will move with them when they move to a different room as toddlers. Cici's sister asks, "What is so hard about your job? You just feed babies and change their diapers."

What could Ceci say in response? Here are some suggestions:

> Talk about how infants' and toddlers' brains grow more quickly in the first three years than at any other time of their lives, and children need responsive interactions to learn. For example, talk about the importance of language development and reading to infants and toddlers.

> Explain that infants' and toddlers' positive emotional and social development provides the foundation for their social *and* academic success in preschool and elementary school. Infants and toddlers need focused attention on their emotional and social development to thrive.

> Talk about the importance of responsive, relationship-based care for infants and toddlers to feel safe to learn.

When you explain the philosophies and research that guide your teaching approach, you'll help families, community members, and others better understand the value of the work you do—and encourage them to partner with you.

Competencies and Standards in Early Childhood Education

Review your professional knowledge and skills with these resources.

NAEYC has developed 10 standards for accreditation of early childhood programs. Families and community agencies recognize NAEYC accreditation as a distinct marker for a quality program. The guide *NAEYC Early Learning Program Accreditation Standards and Assessment Items* (2018) describes the standards in detail, and there are many NAEYC resources to help you through the process of program accreditation. NAEYC.org/accreditation/early-learning/standards

NAEYC's position statement "Professional Standards and Competencies for Early Childhood Educators" outlines what early childhood professionals working with children birth through age 8 should know and be able to do. NAEYC.org/resources /position-statements

Zero to Three's "Critical Competencies for Infant-Toddler Educators" describes the essential knowledge and skills that infant and toddler professionals need. www.zerotothree.org

Caring for Our Children: National Health and Safety Performance Standards: Guidelines for Early Care and Education Programs, 4th edition, covers health promotion, nutrition and food service, infectious diseases, program activities for health development, and more. This book is issued jointly by the American Academy of Pediatrics (AAP), American Public Health Association (APHA) Press, and National Resource Center for Health and Safety in Child Care and Early Education. http://nrckids.org/CFOC

Your profession has developed educator competencies, standards for health and safety, and an accreditation process for early childhood programs. These provide recognition of working with infants and toddlers as a profession with specialized knowledge and skills. The resources listed in the sidebar above support your identity as a professional.

When teachers perceive their job as a long-term career, gain education and experience, and belong to a professional organization such as NAEYC, they create higher-quality programs. These factors influence the quality of teachers' interactions with children (Thomason & La Paro 2013). The quality of teacher–child interactions influences outcomes for children such as their language and cognitive development (Côté et al. 2013).

Challenge *and* Satisfaction

Young children and their families deserve optimal care and learning opportunities. We know that the early years are critical for building children's brain development. The experiences of infants and toddlers in early education settings have the potential to create a solid foundation for children's well-being and success in school and beyond. However, providing responsive, relationship-based care and learning programs is challenging.

There are challenges related to the pay and recognition of infant and toddler professionals. State and federal policies are recognizing the importance of relationship-based programs. Yet there is a continual need to improve policies *and* funding so that programs provide small child-to-staff ratios and decrease the number of children allowed in groups. Teachers may need to think about structural changes in programs in order to better support primary care and continuity of care. Teachers need respectful and responsive ongoing education opportunities to understand the importance of caring relationships and relationship-based practices for young children. Your intensely emotional work with children, families, and other staff is also challenging. Infants and toddlers require mindful, affectionate, and affirmative attention from teachers to thrive.

Working with infants and toddlers, however, is also immensely satisfying. Teachers tell us that they

> Melt when an infant looks up at them with trusting eyes

> Love to see the spark in an infant's eyes when he makes a discovery and then looks to the teacher to share the moment

> Enjoy watching a toddler run excitedly into a room in the morning and straight to a favorite toy

> Appreciate the exploration of a piece of silky cloth by a toddler who shakes it, crumples it, and throws it, listening and looking at the changes she is creating

> Marvel at a toddler who intently focuses to build a tower with blocks while figuring out the dynamics of space and balance

> Understand how important it is when a toddler comforts another toddler

> Know how important they are when a toddler runs pell-mell to them and jumps into their arms when a stranger appears

> Love knowing that thanks to their special, constant helpfulness and the program's responsive philosophy with children and families, children at the age of 3 will have a healthy sense of self-worth that will carry them forth into the world

Professionals Engage in Ethical Practice

Working with infants and toddlers and their families is so important, and a code of ethics helps you act on your commitment to this work.

There is a Code of Ethical Conduct and Statement of Commitment for teachers of children birth to 8 years old (NAEYC 2016). The code describes the core values of the field. It provides guidance for professionals who face conflicting and complex decisions with children and families. For example, what would you do in the following scenario?

> **Zeke (3 months) has just started in a child care program. His teacher, Hailey, tries to be responsive to families' needs. Zeke's parents are recently divorced and his father has primary custody of Zeke. The father usually brings him to the center and picks him up at the end of the day. One day, Zeke's mother stops by the center and asks to see any notes that the teachers have written on Zeke's needs and development. Should Hailey give Zeke's mother the information? What would you do?**

NAEYC's Code of Ethics helps you make a wise decision—an ethical decision. In this case, the principle of doing no harm to children seems to conflict with the principle of not denying family members access to their child's classroom. However, there is an exception. Family members should have access unless the court mandates no access. Here Hailey will need to check in with her director before giving Zeke's mother the information. There are many examples of ethical dilemmas provided by NAEYC (see Feeney & Freeman 2018). These make for exciting and important discussions at staff meetings.

You and Your Well-Being

What other profession includes love, care, and intimacy as part of its work (Page 2018b)? This field requires developing responsive relationships with young children and their families (Honig 2002; Lally & Mangione 2017; Recchia, Shin, & Snaider 2018; Rouse & Hadley 2018; Wittmer & Petersen 2018). We can describe how important positive, caring relationships and sensitive, responsive care are for young children with the term *professional love* (Page 2018a).

Because you must meet children's emotional needs, you need to consider carefully and lovingly your own emotional well-being.

If you are having difficulty comforting an infant or calming a toddler who is having a tantrum, take a few seconds to breathe. Breathe in through your nose for a count of five and hold for a count of four. Then exhale for eight counts through pursed lips while pushing out your belly. This strategy will help calm you so that you can provide the support that infants and toddlers deeply need when they feel out of control.

We hope that you can take time when away from the children in your program to recharge your batteries. When you have a "care for the spirit day" for yourself, you renew your focus on being the responsive, relationship-based teacher you would like to be with very young children.

Teaching in responsive, relationship-based programs is both challenging and satisfying. As a professional, you must take care of your well-being so that you can nurture children and families. Your work results in infants and toddlers who are learning and growing each day in essential ways. You make such a significant and vital difference in children's and families' lives!

This chapter supports the following NAEYC Early Learning Programs standards and topics

Program Standard 6: Staff Competencies, Preparation, and Support
6.B Professional Identity and Recognition
6.D Ongoing Professional Development
Program Standard 8: Community Relationships
8.A Linking with the Community
8.B Accessing Community Resources
8.C Acting as a Citizen in the Neighborhood and the Early Childhood Community
Program Standard 10: Leadership and Management
10.A Leadership

Appendix

Planning Form Around Children's Interests	
Learning area	**Equipment, toys, and materials**
Fine motor/ manipulative	
Large motor/ movement	
Blocks and construction	
Creative	
Sensory experiences	
Reading and literacy	
Dramatic play	
Exploration math and science	
Cozy corners	
Outdoors	
Songs	
Special events (e.g., walks, visitors)	
Families	

References

AAP (American Academy of Pediatrics). 2009. "Abusive Head Trauma: A New Name for Shaken Baby Syndrome." April 27. www.aap.org/en-us/about-the-aap/aap-press-room/Pages/Abusive-Head-Trauma-A-New-Name-for-Shaken-Baby-Syndrome.aspx.

AAP (American Academy of Pediatrics). 2016a. "American Academy of Pediatrics Announces New Recommendations for Children's Media Use." October 21. www.aap.org/en-us/about-the-aap/aap-press-room/Pages/American-Academy-of-Pediatrics-Announces-New-Recommendations-for-Childrens-Media-Use.aspx.

AAP (American Academy of Pediatrics). 2016b. "SIDS and Other Sleep–Related Infant Deaths: Updated 2016 Recommendations for a Safe Infant Sleeping Environment." *Pediatrics* 138 (5): e20162940. https://pediatrics.aappublications.org/content/pediatrics/138/5/e20162938.full.pdf.

AAP (American Academy of Pediatrics). 2017. "Reading With Children Starting in Infancy Gives Lasting Literacy Boost." *AAP News,* May 4. www.aappublications.org/news/2017/05/04/PASLiteracy050417.

Adolph, K.E., W.G. Cole, M. Komati, J.S. Garciaguirre, D. Badaly, J.M. Lingeman, G.L. Chan, & R.B. Sotsky. 2012. "How Do You Learn to Walk? Thousands of Steps and Dozens of Falls per Day." *Psychological Science* 23 (11): 1387–94. https://doi.org/10.1177/0956797612446346.

Afifi, T.O., H.L. MacMillan, M. Boyle, K. Cheung, T. Taillieu, S. Turner, & J. Sareen. 2016. "Child Abuse and Physical Health in Adulthood." *Health Reports* 27 (3): 10–18.

Ainsworth, M.D.S., S.M. Bell, & D.J. Stayton. 1971. "Individual Differences in the Strange Situation Behavior of One-Year-Olds." In *The Origins of Human Social Relations,* ed. H.R. Schaffer, 17–58. San Diego, CA: Academic Press.

APA (American Psychological Association). 2019. "Impact of Physical Discipline on Children May be Harmful in the Long Term, According to APA Resolution." February 18. www.apa.org/news/press/releases/2019/02/physical-discipline.

Badanes, L.S., J. Dmitrieva, & S.E. Watamura. 2012. "Understanding Cortisol Reactivity Across the Day at Child Care: The Potential Buffering Role of Secure Attachment to Caregivers." *Early Childhood Research Quarterly* 27 (1): 156–65. https://doi.org/10.1016/j.ecresq.2011.05.005.

Bakker, M., J.A. Sommerville, & G. Gredebäck. 2016. "Enhanced Neural Processing of Goal-Directed Actions After Active Training in 4-Month-Old Infants." *Journal of Cognitive Neuroscience* 28 (3): 472–82. https://doi.org/10.1162/jocn_a_00909.

Bang, Y. 2014. "Teacher-Caregivers' Perceptions of Toddlers' Adaptation to a Childcare Center." *Social Behavior and Personality: An International Journal* 42 (8): 1279–92. https://doi.org/10.2224/sbp.2014.42.8.1279.

Banks, M. 2018. "Building Relationships with New Families: The Benefits of Gradual Enrollment." Community Playthings, January 23. www.communityplaythings.com/resources/articles/2018/building-relationships-with-new-families.

Beauchamp, G.K., & J.A. Mennella. 2011. "Flavor Perception in Human Infants: Development and Functional Significance." *Digestion* 83 (s1): 1–6. https://doi.org/10.1159/000323397.

Bekker, M.H., M.A. Croon, E.G. van Balkom, & J.B. Vermee. 2008. "Predicting Individual Differences in Autonomy-Connectedness: The Role of Body Awareness, Alexithymia, and Assertiveness." *Journal of Clinical Psychology* 64 (6): 746–65. https://doi.org/10.1002/jclp.20486.

Belsky, J., & R.M. Pasco Fearon. 2002. "Early Attachment Security, Subsequent Maternal Sensitivity, and Later Child Development: Does Continuity in Development Depend upon Continuity of Caregiving?" *Attachment & Human Development* 4 (3): 361–87. https://doi.org/10.1080/14616730210167267.

Bernard, K., E. Peloso, J. Laurenceau, Z. Zhang, & M. Dozier. 2015. "Examining Change in Cortisol Patterns During the 10-Week Transition to a New Child-Care Setting." *Child Development* 86 (2): 456–471. https://doi.org/10.1111/cdev.12304.

Bick, J., T. Zhu, C. Stamoulis, N.A. Fox, C. Zeanah, & C.A. Nelson. 2015. "Effect of Early Institutionalization and Foster Care on Long-Term White Matter Development." *JAMA Pediatrics* 169 (3): 211–19. https://doi.org/10.1001/jamapediatrics.2014.3212.

Biringen, Z. 2008. *The Emotional Availability (EA) Scales, Infancy/Early Childhood Version.* 4th ed. Boulder, CO.

Birmingham, R.S., K.L. Bub, & B.E. Vaughn. 2017. "Parenting in Infancy and Self–Regulation in Preschool: An Investigation of the Role of Attachment History." *Attachment & Human Development* 19 (2): 107–29. https://doi.org/10.1080/14616734.2016.1259335.

Bloom, P. 2017. "Empathy and Its Discontent." *Trends in Cognitive Science* 21 (1): 24–31. https://doi.org/10.1016/j.tics.2016.11.004.

Boldt, L.J., G. Kochanska, J.E. Yoon, & J.K. Nordling. 2014. "Children's Attachment to Both Parents from Toddler Age to Middle Childhood: Links to Adaptive and Maladaptive Outcomes." *Attachment & Human Development* 16 (3): 211–29. https://doi.org/10.1080/14616734.2014.889181.

Booth-LaForce, C., A.M. Groh, M.R. Burchinal, G.I. Roisman, M.T. Owen, & M.J. Cox. 2014. "Caregiving and Contextual Sources of Continuity and Change in Attachment Security from Infancy to Late Adolescence." *Monographs of the Society for Research in Child Development* 79 (3): 67–84. https://doi.org/10.1111/mono.12114.

Bowlby, J. 1980. *Attachment and Loss*, Vol. 3: *Loss: Sadness and Depression*. New York: Basic Books.

Brock, R. L., & Kochanska, G. 2019. "Anger In Infancy And Its Implications: History Of Attachment In Mother-Child and Father-Child Relationships As A Moderator Of Risk." *Development & Psychopathology,* 31 (4): 1353-66. doi:10.1017/S0954579418000780.

Bronfenbrenner, U., ed. 2005. *Making Human Beings Human: Bioecological Perspectives on Human Development*. Thousand Oaks, CA: Sage.

Brooker, I., & D. Poulin-Dubois. 2013. "Is a Bird an Apple? The Effect of Speaker Labeling Accuracy on Infants' World Learning, Imitation, and Helping Behaviors." *Infancy* 18 (s1): E46–E68. https://doi.org/10.1111/infa.12027.

Brophy-Herb, H.E., R.F. Schiffman, E.L. Bocknek, S.B. Dupuis, H.E. Fitzgerald, M. Horodynski, E. Onaga, L.A. Van Egeren, & B. Hillaker. 2011. "Toddlers' Social-Emotional Competence in the Contexts of Maternal Emotion Socialization and Contingent Responsiveness in a Low-Income Sample." *Social Development* 20 (1): 73–92. https://doi.org/10.1111/j.1467-9507.2009.00570.x.

Brophy-Herb, H.E., E.L. Bocknek, C.D. Vallotton, K.E. Stansbury, N. Senehi, D. Dalimonte-Merckling, & Y. Lee. 2015. "Toddlers With Early Behavioral Problems at Higher Family Demographic Risk Benefit the Most From Maternal Emotion Talk." *Journal of Developmental & Behavioral Pediatrics* 36 (7): 512–20. https://doi.org/10.1097/DBP.0000000000000196.

Brown, R. 1973. *A First Language: The Early Stages*. London: George Allen & Unwin.

Brownfield, K., & I.A.G. Wilkinson. 2018. "Examining the Impact of Scaffolding on Literacy Learning: A Critical Examination of Research and Guidelines to Advance Inquiry." *International Journal of Educational Research* 90: 177–90. https://doi.org/10.1016/j.ijer.2018.01.004.

Brumariu, L.E., & K.A. Kerns. 2013. "Pathways to Anxiety: Contributions of Attachment History, Temperament, Peer Competence, and Ability to Manage Intense Emotions." *Child Psychiatry & Human Development* 44 (4): 504–15. https://doi.org/10.1007/s10578-012-0345-7.

Bruner, J.S. 1978. "The Role of Dialogue in Language Acquisition." In *The Child's Conception of Language*, eds. A. Sinclair, R.J. Jarvella, & W.J.M. Levelt, 241–56. New York: Springer-Verlag.

Cassidy, J., & P.R. Shaver. eds. 2016. *Handbook of Attachment: Theory, Research, and Clinical Application,* 3rd ed. York, PA: Guilford Press.

CDC (Centers for Disease Control and Prevention). 2019. "What Is Autism Spectrum Disorder?" Last reviewed August 27, 2019. www.cdc.gov/ncbddd/autism/facts.html.

CDC (Centers for Disease Control and Prevention). 2020. "Early Brain Development and Health." Last reviewed March 5, 2020. www.cdc.gov/ncbddd/childdevelopment/early -brain-development.html.

Center on the Developing Child. n.d. a. "Brain Architecture." Harvard University. Accessed February 17, 2019. www.developingchild .harvard.edu/science/key-concepts/brain -architecture.

Center on the Developing Child. n.d. b. "Serve and Return." Harvard University. Accessed February 17, 2019. www.developingchild.harvard .edu/science/key-concepts/serve-and-return.

Cheeseman, S. 2017. "Narratives of Infants' Encounters With Curriculum: Beyond the Curriculum of Care." *Contemporary Issues in Early Childhood* 18 (1): 55–66. https://doi .org/10.1177/1463949117692243.

Chen, X. 2018. "Culture, Temperament, and Social and Psychological Adjustment." *Developmental Review* 50: 42–53. https://doi.org/10.1016/j.dr.2018.03.004.

Child Welfare Information Gateway. 2019. *Long-Term Consequences of Child Abuse and Neglect*. Fact sheet. Washington, DC: US Department of Health and Human Services, Administration for Children and Families, Children's Bureau. www.childwelfare.gov /pubpdfs/long_term_consequences.pdf.

Choi, J.Y., D. Horm, & S. Jeon. 2018. "Descriptive Study of Continuity of Care Practice and Children's Experience of Stability of Care in Early Head Start." *Child & Youth Care Forum* 47 (5): 659–81. https://doi.org/10.1007 /s10566-018-9450-5.

Colorado Office of Early Childhood. n.d. "Expanding Quality in Infant Toddler Care Initiative." Accessed February 17, 2019. coloradoofficeofearlychildhood.force.com /oec/OEC_Providers?p=Providers&s =Expanding-Quality-in-Infant-Toddler -Care-Initiative&lang=en.

Côté, S.M., C. Mongeau, C. Japel, Q. Xu, J.R. Séguin, & R.E. Tremblay. 2013. "Child Care Quality and Cognitive Development: Trajectories Leading to Better Preacademic Skills." *Child Development* 84 (2): 752–66. https://doi.org/10.1111/cdev.12007.

CRC (The Convention on the Rights of the Child). n.d. "About the Convention." Accessed February 17, 2019. https://static.unicef.org /rightsite/237_202.htm.

Crivello, C., O. Kuzyk, M. Rodrigues, M. Friend, P. Zesiger, & D. Poulin-Dubois. 2016. "The Effects of Bilingual Growth on Toddlers' Executive Function." *Journal of Experimental Child Psychology* 141: 121–32. https://doi .org/10.1016/j.jecp.2015.08.004.

Cuevas, K., K. Deater-Deckard, J. Kim-Spoon, A.J. Watson, K.C. Morasch, & M.A. Bell. 2014. "What's Mom Got to Do with It? Contributions of Maternal Executive Function and Caregiving to the Development of Executive Function Across Early Childhood." *Developmental Science* 17 (2): 224–38. https://doi.org/10.1111/desc.12073.

Degotardi, S. 2017. "Joint Attention in Infant– Toddler Early Childhood Programs: Its Dynamics and Potential for Collaborative Learning." *Contemporary Issues in Early Childhood* 18 (4): 409–21. https://doi.org /10.1177/1463949117742786.

Degotardi, S., J. Torr, & A. Nguyen. 2016. "Infant–Toddler Educators' Language Support Practices During Snack-Time." *Australasian Journal of Early Childhood* 41 (4): 52–62.

Degotardi, S., J. Page, & E.J. White. 2017. "(Re) conceptualising Relationships in Infant– Toddler Pedagogy." *Contemporary Issues in Early Childhood* 18 (4): 355–61. https://doi .org/10.1177/1463949117742760.

de Groot Kim, S. 2010. "There's Elly, It Must Be Tuesday: Discontinuity in Child Care Programs and Its Impact on the Development of Peer Relationships in Young Children." *Early Childhood Education Journal* 38 (2): 153–164. https://doi.org/10.1007/s10643-010-0400-6.

Dempsey-Jones, H. 2017. "Touch in Infancy is Important for Healthy Brain Development." *The Conversation*, March 23. www.theconversation.com/touch-in-infancy-is-important-for-healthy-brain-development-74864.

de Schipper, E.J., M. Riksen-Walraven, & A.E.G. Sabine. 2006. "Effects of Child–Caregiver Ratio on the Interactions Between Caregivers and Children in Child Care Centers: An Experimental Study." *Child Development* 77: 861–64.

de Villiers Rader, N., & P. Zukow-Goldring. 2012. "Caregivers' Gestures Direct Infant Attention During Early Word Learning: The Importance of Dynamic Synchrony." *Language Sciences* 34 (5): 559–68. https://doi.org/10.1016/j.langsci.2012.03.011.

Dewar, G. n.d. "The Newborn Senses: What Can Babies Feel, See, Hear, Smell, and Taste?" Accessed February 17, 2019. www.parentingscience.com/newborn-senses.html.

DiCarlo, C.F., C. Onwujuba, & J.I. Baumgartner. 2014. "Infant Communicative Behaviors and Maternal Responsiveness." *Child & Youth Care Forum* 43 (2): 195–209. https://doi.org/10.1007/s10566-013-9233-y.

Ebbeck, M., D.M.Y. Phoon, E. Tan-Chong, M.A.B. Tan, & M.L.M. Goh. 2015. "A Research Study on Secure Attachment Using the Primary Caregiving Approach." *Early Childhood Education Journal* 43 (3): 233–40. https://doi.org/10.1007/s10643-014-0647-4.

Ebbeck, M., S. Warrier, & M. Goh. 2018. "Early Experiences Matter: A Relationships-Based Curriculum for the Birth-to-Three Age Group." *Early Childhood Education Journal* 46 (1): 83–92. https://doi.org/10.1007/s10643-017-0847-9.

Engle, J.M., & N.L. McElwain. 2011. "Parental Reactions to Toddlers' Negative Emotions and Child Negative Emotionality as Correlates of Problem Behavior at the Age of Three." *Social Development* 20 (2): 251–71. https://doi.org/10.1111/j.1467-9507.2010.00583.x.

Feeney, S., & N.K. Freeman. 2018. *Ethics and the Early Childhood Educator: Using the NAEYC Code.* 3rd ed. Washington, DC: NAEYC.

Feldman, R., M. Singer, & O. Zagoory. 2010. "Touch Attenuates Infants' Physiological Reactivity to Stress." *Developmental Science* 13 (2): 271–78. https://doi.org/10.1111/j.1467-7687.2009.00890.x.

Feldman, R., E. Bamberger, & Y. Kanat-Maymon. 2013. "Parent-Specific Reciprocity from Infancy to Adolescence Shapes Children's Social Competence and Dialogical Skills." *Attachment & Human Development* 15 (4): 407–23. https://doi.org/10.1080/14616734.2013.782650.

Fernald, A. 1993. "Approval and Disapproval: Infant Responsiveness to Vocal Affect in Familiar and Unfamiliar Languages." *Child Development* 64 (3): 657–74. https://doi.org/10.2307/1131209.

Fink, C., & M. Marxer. n.d. "10 Ways Babies Learn When We Sing to Them." NAEYC. Accessed March 15, 2019. www.naeyc.org/our-work/families/10-ways-babies-learn-sing-to-them.

Folsom, J.S. 2017. "Dialogic Reading: Having a Conversation About Books." Iowa Reading Research Center, January 3. www.iowareadingresearch.org/blog/dialogic-reading-having-a-conversation-about-books.

Forestell, C.A., & J.A Mennella. 2007. "Early Determinants of Fruit And Vegetable Acceptance." *Pediatric* 120: 1247–54. https://doi.org/10.1542/peds.2007-0858.

Fox, N.A., T.V. Barker, L.K. White, J.G. Suway, & D.S. Pine. 2013. "Commentary: To Intervene or Not? Appreciating or Treating Individual Differences in Childhood Temperament—Remarks on Rapee." *Journal of Child Psychology and Psychiatry* 54 (7): 789–90. https://doi.org/10.1111/jcpp.12101.

Gandini, L., & J. Goldhaber. 2001. "Two Reflections About Documentation." In *Bambini: The Italian Approach to Infant/Toddler Care,* eds. L. Gandini & C.P. Edwards, 124–45. New York: Teachers College Press.

Garrity, S., S. Longstreth, & M. Alwashmi. 2016. "A Qualitative Examination of the Implementation of Continuity of Care: An Organizational Learning Perspective." *Early Childhood Research Quarterly* 36: 64–78. https://doi.org/10.1016/j.ecresq .2015.12.014.

Gensthaler, A., E. Möhler, F. Resch, F. Paulus, C. Schwenck, C.M. Freitag, & K. Goth. 2013. "Retrospective Assessment of Behavioral Inhibition in Infants and Toddlers: Development of a Parent Report Questionnaire." *Child Psychiatry & Human Development* 44 (1): 152–65. https://doi .org/10.1007/s10578-012-0316-z.

Gibson, J.J. [1979] 1986. *The Ecological Approach to Visual Perception.* Hillsdale, NJ: Lawrence Erlbaum Associates.

Gillespie, L.G. 2015. "Rocking and Rolling— It Takes Two: The Role of Co-Regulation in Building Self-Regulation Skills." *Young Children* 70 (3): 94–96. www.naeyc.org /resources/pubs/yc/jul2015/rocking-rolling.

Gillespie, L.G. 2016. "Rocking and Rolling: It's Never 'Just Play'!" *Young Children* 71 (3): 92–94. https://www.naeyc.org/resources /pubs/yc/jul2016/rocking-rolling.

Gillespie, L.G., & J.D. Greenberg. 2017. "Rocking and Rolling: Empowering Infants' and Toddlers' Learning Through Scaffolding." *Young Children* 72 (2): 90–93. www.naeyc .org/resources/pubs/yc/may2017/rocking-and -rolling-empowering-infants-and-toddlers.

Gloeckler, L., & J. Cassell. 2012. "Teacher Practices With Toddlers During Social Problem Solving Opportunities." *Early Childhood Education Journal* 40 (4): 251–57. https://doi .org/10.1007/s10643-011-0495-4.

Goldstein, M.H., & J.A. Schwade. 2008. "Social Feedback to Infants' Babbling Facilitates Rapid Phonological Learning." *Psychological Science* 19 (5): 515–23. https://doi.org/10.1111 /j.1467-9280.2008.02117.x.

Grady, J. S., & Callan, D. 2019. "Shy Toddlers Act Bold: The Roles of Respiratory Sinus Arrhythmia and Parent Emotion Language." *Infant Behavior and Development* 55: 32-37. https://doi.org/10.1016/j.infbeh .2019.02.005

Grazzani, I., V. Ornaghi, A. Agliati, & E. Brazzelli. 2016. "How to Foster Toddlers' Mental-State Talk, Emotion Understanding, and Prosocial Behavior: A Conversation-Based Intervention at Nursery School." *Infancy* 21 (2): 199–227. https://doi.org/10.1111/infa.12107.

Greenberg, J. 2012. "Rocking and Rolling: More, All Gone, Empty, Full: Math Talk Every Day in Every Way." *Young Children* 67 (3): 62–64.

Groh, A.M., R. Pasco Fearon, M.J. Bakermans- Kranenburg, M.H. van IJzendoorn, R.D. Steele, & G.I. Roisman. 2014. "The Significance of Attachment Security for Children's Social Competence with Peers: A Meta-Analytic Study." *Attachment & Human Development* 16 (2): 103–36. https://doi.org/10.1080 /14616734.2014.883636.

Hallam, R.A., H.N. Fouts, K.N. Bargreen, & K. Perkins. 2016. "Teacher–Child Interactions During Mealtimes: Observations of Toddlers in High Subsidy Child Care Settings." *Early Childhood Education Journal* 44 (1): 51–59. https://doi.org/10.1007/s10643-014-0678-x.

Hammer, C.S., P. Morgan, G. Farkas, M. Hillemeier, D. Bitetti, & S. Maczuga. 2017. "Late Talkers: A Population-Based Study of Risk Factors and School Readiness Consequences." *Journal of Speech, Language, and Hearing Research* 60 (3): 607–26. https://doi.org/10.1044/2016 _JSLHR-L-15-0417.

Hay, D.F., C.S. Waters, O. Perra, N. Swift, V. Kairis, R. Phillips, R. Jones, I. Goodyer, G. Harold, A. Thapar, & S. van Goozen. 2014. "Precursors to Aggression are Evident by 6 Months of Age." *Developmental Science* 17 (3): 471–80. https://doi.org/10.1111 /desc.12133.

Hay, J.F., B. Pelucchi, K.G. Estes, & J.R. Saffran. 2011. "Linking Sounds to Meanings: Infant Statistical Learning in a Natural Language." *Cognitive Psychology* 63 (2): 93–106. https://doi.org/10.1016/j.cogpsych.2011.06.002.

Hedenbro, M., & P. Rydelius. 2014. "Early Interaction Between Infants and Their Parents Predicts Social Competence at the Age of Four." *Acta Paediatrica* 103 (3): 268–74. https://doi.org/10.1111/apa.12512.

Hepach, R., A. Vaish, & M. Tomasello. 2013. "A New Look at Children's Prosocial Motivation." In "Early Development of Prosocial Behavior," ed. C.A. Brown, special issue, *Infancy* 18 (1): 67–90. https://doi.org/10.1111/j.1532-7078.2012.00130.x.

Hepach, R., A. Vaish, & M. Tomasello. 2017. "Children's Intrinsic Motivation to Provide Help Themselves After Accidentally Harming Others." *Child Development* 88 (4): 1251–64. https://doi.org/10.1111/cdev.12646.

Hilbrink, E.E., E. Sakkalou, K. Ellis-Davies, N.C. Fowler, & M. Gattis. 2013. "Selective and Faithful Imitation at 12 and 15 Months." *Developmental Science* 16 (6): 828–40. https://doi.org/10.1111/desc.12070.

Hilman, C.B. 2012. "The Intangibles in the Early Childhood Classroom." *Exchange* (March/April): 12–14. http://mail.ccie.com/library/5020412.pdf.

Holvoet, C., C. Scola, T. Arciszewski, & D. Picard. 2016. "Infants' Preference for Prosocial Behaviors: A Literature Review." *Infant Behavior and Development* 45 (part B): 125–139. https://doi.org/10.1016/j.infbeh.2016.10.008.

Honig, A.S. 1982. *Playtime Learning Games for Young Children*. Syracuse, NY: Syracuse University Press.

Honig, A.S. 2001. "Language Flowering: Language Empowering: 20 Ways Parents Can Assist Young Children." *Montessori Life* 13 (4): 31–35.

Honig, A.S. 2002. *Secure Relationships: Nurturing Infant/Toddler Attachment in Early Care Settings*. Washington, DC: NAEYC.

Honig, A.S. 2005. "The Language of Lullabies." In *Spotlight on Young Children and the Creative Arts,* ed. D. Koralek, 4–5. Washington, DC: NAEYC.

Honig, A.S. 2014. *The Best for Babies: Expert Advices for Caregivers and Administrators in Assessing Infant–Toddler Programs*. Lewisville, NC: Gryphon House.

Honig, A.S. 2015. *Experiencing Nature with Young Children: Awakening Delight, Curiosity, and a Sense of Stewardship*. Washington, DC: NAEYC.

Honig, A.S. 2020. *Tuning Into Infants and Toddlers: Positive Behavior Guidance*. Little Rock, AR: Southern Early Childhood Association.

Honig, A.S., & M. Shin. 2001. "Reading Aloud to Infants and Toddlers in Child Care Settings: An Observational Study." *Early Childhood Education Journal* 28 (3): 193–97. https://doi.org/10.1023/A:1026551403754.

Hopwood-Stephens, I. 2015. *Outdoor Play for 1–3 Year Olds: How to Set Up and Run Your Own Outdoor Toddler Group*. London: Routledge.

Horm, D., D. Norris, D. Perry, R. Chazan-Cohen, & T. Halle. 2016. *Developmental Foundations of School Readiness for Infants and Toddlers: A Research to Practice Report*. OPRE Report # 2016–07. Washington, DC: OPRE.

Howes, C. 1996. "The Earliest Friendships." In *The Company They Keep: Friendship in Childhood and Adolescence*, eds. W.M. Bukowski, A.F. Newcomb, & W.W. Hartup, 66–86. New York: Cambridge University Press.

Howes, C., & S. Spieker. 2008. "Attachment Relationships in the Context of Multiple Caregivers." In *Handbook of Attachment: Theory, Research, and Clinical Applications*, eds. J. Cassidy & P.R. Shaver, 317–32. New York: Guilford Press.

Huang, J., Y. Kim, M. Sherraden, & M. Clancy. 2017. "Unmarried Mothers and Children's Social-Emotional Development: The Role of Child Development Accounts." *Journal of Child and Family Studies* 26 (1): 234–47. https://doi.org/10.1007/s10826-016-0551-1.

Hymel, S., & L. Ford. 2014. "School Completion and Academic Success: The Impact of Early Social-Emotional Competence." *Encyclopedia on Early Child Development*. www.child-encyclopedia.com/sites/default/files/textes-experts/en/839/school-completion-and-academic-success-the-impact-of-early-social-emotional-competence.pdf.

Isik-Ercan, Z. 2017. "Culturally Appropriate Positive Guidance with Young Children." *Young Children* 72 (1): 15–21. www.naeyc.org/resources/pubs/yc/mar2017/culturally-appropriate-positive-guidance.

Jenni, O.G., A. Chaouch, J. Caflisch, & V. Rousson. 2013. "Infant Motor Milestones: Poor Predictive Value for Outcome of Healthy Children." *Acta Paediatrica* 102 (4): e181–e184. https://doi.org/10.1111/apa.12129.

Jung, J., & S. Recchia. 2013. "Scaffolding Infants' Play Through Empowering and Individualizing Teaching Practices." *Early Education and Development* 24 (6): 829–50. https://doi.org/10.1080/10409289.2013.744683.

Kagan, J., & N. Snidman. 2009. *The Long Shadow of Temperament*. Boston: Belknap Press.

Kaplan, L.J. 1978. *Oneness and Separateness: From Infant to Individual*. New York: Touchstone.

Kapsimali, M., & L.A. Barlow. 2013. "Developing a Sense of Taste." *Seminars in Cell and Developmental Biology* 24 (3): 200–209. https://doi.org/10.1016/j.semcdb.2012.11.002.

Kerns, K.A., & L.E. Brumariu. 2014. "Is Insecure Parent-Child Attachment a Risk Factor for the Development of Anxiety in Childhood or Adolescence?" *Child Development Perspectives* 8 (1): 12–17. doi:10.1111/cdep.12054

Kibbe, M.M., & A.M. Leslie. 2011. "What Do Infants Remember When They Forget? Location and Identity in 6-Month-Olds' Memory for Objects." *Psychological Science* 22 (12): 1500–1505. https://doi.org/10.1177/0956797611420165.

Kiel, E.J., J.E. Premo, & K.A. Buss. 2016. "Maternal Encouragement to Approach Novelty: A Curvilinear Relation to Change in Anxiety for Inhibited Toddlers." *Journal of Abnormal Child Psychology* 44 (3): 433–44. https://doi.org/10.1007/s10802-015-0038-3.

Kiley Hamlin, J., & K. Wynn. 2011. "Young Infants Prefer Prosocial to Antisocial Others." *Cognitive Development* 26 (1): 30–39. https://doi.org/10.1016/j.cogdev.2010.09.001.

Kim, S., & G. Kochanska. 2015. "Mothers' Power Assertion; Children's Negative, Adversarial Orientation; and Future Behavior Problems in Low-Income Families: Early Maternal Responsiveness as a Moderator of the Developmental Cascade." *Journal of Family Psychology* 29 (1): 1–9. https://doi.org/10.1037/a0038430.

Kim. S., H. Im, & K. Kwon. 2015. "The Role of Home Literacy Environment in Toddlerhood in Development of Vocabulary and Decoding Skills." *Child & Youth Care Forum*. 44 (6): 835–52. https://doi.org/10.1007/s10566-015-9309-y.

Kirk, E., N. Howlett, K.J. Pine, & B. Fletcher. 2013. "To Sign or Not to Sign? The Impact of Encouraging Infants to Gesture on Infant Language and Maternal Mind-Mindedness." *Child Development* 84 (2): 574590. https://doi.org/10.1111/j.1467-8624.2012.01874.x.

Kirk, E., K. Pine, L. Wheatley, N. Howlett, J. Schulz, & B. Fletcher. 2015. "A Longitudinal Investigation of the Relationship Between Maternal Mind-Mindedness and Theory of Mind." *British Journal of Developmental Psychology* 33 (4): 434–45. https://doi.org/10.1111/bjdp.12104.

Kirkorian, H.L., K. Choi, & T.A. Pempek. 2016. "Toddlers' Word Learning From Contingent and Noncontingent Video on Touch Screens." *Child Development* 87 (2): 405–13. https://doi.org/10.1111/cdev.12508.

Klein, P.S., & R. Feldman. 2007. "Mothers' and Caregivers' Interactive and Teaching Behavior with Toddlers." *Early Child Development and Care* 177 (4): 383–402.

Kleppe, R. 2018. "Affordances for 1- to 3-Year-Olds' Risky Play in Early Childhood Education and Care." *Journal of Early Childhood Research* 16 (3): 258–75. https://doi.org/10.1080/03004430600551682.

Kluger, J. 2013. "The Power of the Bilingual Brain." *Time,* July 29. www.time.com/595/the-power-of-the-bilingual-brain.

Knudsen, B., & U. Liszkowski. 2013. "One-Year-Olds Warn Others About Negative Action Outcomes." *Journal of Cognition and Development* 14 (3): 424–36. https://doi.org/10.1080/15248372.2012.689387.

Kok, R., M.H. van IJzendoorn, M. Linting, M.J. Bakermans–Kranenburg, A. Tharner, M.P.C.M. Luijk, E. Szèkely, V.W.V Jaddoe, A. Hofman, F.C. Verhulst, & H. Tiemeier. 2013. "Attachment Insecurity Predicts Child Active Resistance to Parental Requests in a Compliance Task." *Child: Care, Health and Development* 39 (2): 277–87. https://doi.org/10.1111/j.1365-2214.2012.01374.x.

Koralek, D., K. Nemeth, & K. Ramsey. 2019. *Families & Educators Together: Building Great Relationships that Support Young Children.* Washington, DC: NAEYC.

Köster, M., X. Ohmer, T.D. Nguyen, & J. Kärtner. 2016. "Infants Understand Others' Needs." *Psychological Science* 27 (4): 542–48. https://doi.org/10.1177/0956797615627426.

Kovach, B., & D. Da Ros-Voseles. 2008. *Being with Babies: Understanding and Responding to the Infants in Your Care.* Beltsville, MD: Gryphon House.

Kuhl, P.K. 2007. "Is Speech Learning 'Gated' by the Social Brain?" *Developmental Science* 10 (1): 110–120. doi:10.1111/j.1467-7687.2007.00572.x.

Kuhl, P.K., F.M. Tsao, & H.M. Liu. 2003. "Foreign-Language Experience in Infancy: Effects of Short-Term Exposure and Social Interaction on Phonetic Learning." *Proceedings of the National Academy of Sciences of the United States of America* 100 (15): 9096–101. https://doi.org/10.1073/pnas.1532872100

Lally, J.R. 2014. "The Human Brain's Need for a 'Social Womb' During Infancy." *For Our Babies,* April 15. forourbabies.org/wp-content/uploads/2014/04/The-Human-Brains-Need-for-a-Social-WombFINAL April2014.pdf.

Lally, J.R., Y.L. Torres, & P.C. Phelps. 2010. "How to Care for Infants and Toddlers in Groups." *ZERO TO THREE,* February 8. www.zerotothree.org/resources/77-how-to-care-for-infants-and-toddlers-in-groups.

Lally, J.R., & P.L. Mangione. 2017. "Caring Relationships: The Heart of Early Brain Development." *Young Children* 72 (2): 17–24. www.naeyc.org/resources/pubs/yc/may2017/caring-relationships-heart-early-brain-development.

Lang, S.N., A.R. Tolbert, S.J. Schoppe-Sullivan, & A.E. Bonomi. 2016. "A Cocaring Framework for Infants and Toddlers: Applying a Model of Coparenting to Parent–Teacher Relationships." *Early Childhood Research Quarterly* 34 (1): 40–52. https://doi.org/10.1016/j.ecresq.2015.08.004.

Laurin, D.E., & C.B. Goble. 2018. "Enhancing the Diapering Routine: Caring, Communication, and Development." *Young Children* 73 (3): 18–25. https://doi.org/10.1002/jcop.21602.

Lickenbrock, D.M., J.M. Braungart–Rieker, N.V. Ekas, S.R. Zentall, T. Oshio, & E.M. Planalp. 2013. "Early Temperament and Attachment Security with Mothers and Fathers as Predictors of Toddler Compliance and Noncompliance." *Infant & Child Development* 22 (6): 580–602. https://doi.org/10.1002/icd.1808.

Lieberman, A.F. 2017. *The Emotional Life of the Toddler.* New York: Simon & Schuster.

Løkken, G. 2000. "The Playful Quality of the Toddling 'Style.'" *International Journal of Qualitative Studies in Education* 13 (5): 531–42. https://doi.org/10.1080/09518390050156440.

Lorber, M.F., & B. Egeland. 2011. "Parenting and Infant Difficulty: Testing a Mutual Exacerbation Hypothesis to Predict Early Onset Conduct Problems." *Child Development* 82 (6): 2006–20. https://doi.org/10.1111/j.1467-8624.2011.01652.x.

Luckenbill, J. n.d. "11 Ways to Help Children Say Goodbye." Accessed January 23, 2019. www.naeyc.org/our-work/families/help-children-say-goodbye.

Luckenbill, J., A. Subramaniam, & J. Thompson. 2019. *This Is Play: Environments and Interactions that Engage Infants and Toddlers.* Washington, DC: NAEYC.

Maclaughlin, S. 2017. "Rocking and Rolling. Reflection: The First Step for Addressing Bias in Infant and Toddler Programs." *Young Children* 72 (5) 90–93. www.naeyc.org/resources/pubs/yc/nov2017/rocking-and-rolling.

Madigan, S., D. Browne, N. Racine, C. Mori, & S. Tough. 2019. "Association Between Screen Time and Children's Performance on a Developmental Screening Test." *JAMA Pediatrics* 173 (3): 244–50. https://doi.org/10.1001/jamapediatrics.2018.5056.

Mahler, M., F. Pine, & A. Bergman. [1975] 2000. *The Psychological Birth of The Human Infant.* New York: Basic Books.

Maslow, A.H. 1987. *Motivation and Personality.* 3rd ed. New York: Harper & Row.

Mayor, J., & K. Plunkett. 2014. "Shared Understanding and Idiosyncratic Expression in Early Vocabularies." *Developmental Science* 17 (3): 412–23. https://doi.org/10.1111/desc.12130.

McCord, S. 2011. *The Storybook Journey: Pathways to Learning Through Story and Play.* CreateSpace Independent Publishing.

McElwain, N.L., C. Booth-LaForce, J.E. Lansford, X. Wu, & W.J. Dyer. 2008. "A Process Model of Attachment-Friend Linkages: Hostile Attribution Biases, Language Ability, and Mother-Child Affective Mutuality as Intervening Mechanisms." *Child Development* 79 (6): 1891–1906. https://doi.org/10.1111/j.1467-8624.2008.01232.x.

McElwain, N.L., A.S. Holland, J.M. Engle, & B.G. Ogolsky. 2014. "Getting Acquainted: Actor and Partner Effects of Attachment and Temperament on Young Children's Peer Behavior." *Developmental Psychology* 50 (6): 1757–70. doi:10.1037/a0036211.

McMullen, M.B. 2017. "Continuity of Care with Infants and Toddlers." *Exchange* (January/February): 43–50.

McMullen, M.B., J.M. Addleman, A.M. Fulford, S.L. Moore, S.J. Mooney, S.S. Sisk, & J. Zachariah. 2009. "Learning to Be *Me* While Coming to Understand *We*: Encouraging Proscocial Babies in Group Settings." *Young Children* 64 (4): 20–27.

Meins, E. 2013. "Sensitive Attunement to Infants' Internal States: Operationalizing the Construct of Mind-Mindedness." *Attachment & Human Development* 15 (5–6): 524–44. https://doi.org/10.1080/14616734.2013.830388.

Meins, E., L.C. Muñoz Centifanti, C. Fernyhough, & S. Fishburn. 2013. "Maternal Mind-Mindedness and Children's Behavioral Difficulties: Mitigating the Impact of Low Socioeconomic Status." *Journal of Abnormal Child Psychology* 41 (4): 543–53. https://doi.org/10.1007/s10802-012-9699-3.

Mermelshtine, R., & J. Barnes. 2016. "Maternal Responsive-Didactic Caregiving in Play Interactions with 10-Month-Olds and Cognitive Development at 18 Months." *Infant & Child Development* 25 (3): 296–316. https://doi.org/10.1002/icd.1961.

Mesman, J., T. Minter, & A. Angnged. 2016. "Received Sensitivity: Adapting Ainsworth's Scale to Capture Sensitivity in a Multiple-Caregiver Context." *Attachment & Human Development* 18 (2): 101–114. https://doi.org/10.1080/14616734.2015.1133681.

Mitchelmore, S., S. Degotardi, & A. Fleet. 2017. "The Richness of Everyday Moments: Bringing Visibility to the Qualities of Care Within Pedagogical Spaces." In *Under-Three Year Olds in Policy and Practice,* eds. E.J. White & C. Dalli, 87–99. Singapore: Springer.

Moding, K.J., & C.A. Stifter. 2018. "Does Temperament Underlie Infant Novel Food Responses? Continuity of Approach–Withdrawal From 6 to 18 Months." *Child Development* 89 (4): e444-e458.

MOE (Ministry of Education). 2004. *Kei Tua o te Pae: Assessment for Learning: Early Childhood Exemplars*. Wellington, NZ: Learning Media Limited. www.education.govt .nz/assets/Documents/Early-Childhood /Kei-Tua-o-te-Pae/ECEBooklet8Full.pdf.

Moffitt, T.E., L. Arseneault, D. Belsky, N. Dickson, R.J. Hancox, H. Harrington, R. Houts, R. Poulton, B.W. Roberts, S. Ross, M.R. Sears, W.M. Thomson, & A. Caspi. 2011. "A Gradient of Childhood Self-Control Predicts Health, Wealth, and Public Safety." *Proceedings of the National Academy of Sciences of the United States of America* 108 (7): 2693–98. https://doi.org/10.1073/pnas.1010076108.

Moran, K.M., N.A. Turiano, & A.L. Gentzler. 2018. "Parental Warmth During Childhood Predicts Coping and Well-Being in Adulthood." *Journal of Family Psychology* 32 (5): 610–21.

Morgan, P.L., G. Farkas, M.M. Hillemeier, C.S. Hammer, & S. Maczuga. 2015. "24-Month-Old Children with Larger Oral Vocabularies Display Greater Academic and Behavioral Functioning at Kindergarten Entry." *Child Development* 86 (5): 1351–70. https://doi.org/10.1111 /cdev.12398.

Mortensen, J.A., & M.A. Barnett. 2015. "Teacher–Child Interactions in Infant/Toddler Child Care and Socioemotional Development." *Early Education and Development* 26 (2): 209–29. https://doi.org/10.1080/10409289 .2015.985878.

Mortlock, A. 2015. "Toddlers' Use of Peer Rituals at Mealtime: Symbols of Togetherness and Otherness." *International Journal of Early Years Education* 23 (4): 426–35. https://doi .org/10.1080/09669760.2015.1096237.

Moullin, S., J. Waldfogel, & E. Washbrook. 2017. "Parent-Child Attachment as A Mechanism of Intergeneration (Dis)Advantage." *Families, Relationships and Societies* 7 (2): 265–84. https://scholar.princeton.edu/sites/default /files/smoullin/files/frs_ft_moullin_uploaded _061017.pdf.

NAEYC. 2016. *Code of Ethical Conduct and Statement of Commitment*. Brochure. Rev. ed. Washington, DC: NAEYC. www.naeyc.org /positionstatements/ethical_conduct.

NAEYC. 2018. *Early Learning Program Accreditation Standards and Assessment Items*. Washington, DC: NAEYC. www.naeyc .org/accreditation/early-learning/standards.

NAEYC. 2019. "Professional Standards and Competencies for Early Childhood Educators." Position statement. Washington, DC: NAEYC. www.naeyc.org/resources/position-statements /professional-standards-competencies.

NAEYC. n.d. a. "3 Core Considerations." Accessed January 10, 2019. www.naeyc.org/resources /topics/dap/3-core-considerations.

NAEYC. n.d. b. "Math Talk with Infants and Toddlers." Accessed March 23, 2019. www.naeyc.org/our-work/families/math-talk -infants-and-toddlers.

Nell, M.L., & W.F. Drew. n.d. "Five Essentials to Meaningful Play." NAEYC. Accessed February 5, 2019. www.naeyc.org/our-work /families/five-essentials-meaningful-play.

NSCDC (National Scientific Council on the Developing Child). 2010. "Persistent Fear and Anxiety Can Affect Young Children's Learning and Development." Working Paper 9. February. https://developingchild.harvard.edu/wp -content/uploads/2010/05/Persistent-Fear -and-Anxiety-Can-Affect-Young-Childrens -Learning-and-Development.pdf.

NSCDC (National Scientific Council on the Developing Child). 2014. "Excessive Stress Disrupts the Architecture of the Developing Brain." Working Paper 3. Updated edition. January. https://developingchild.harvard .edu/wp-content/uploads/2005/05/Stress _Disrupts_Architecture_Developing _Brain-1.pdf.

NSF (National Science Foundation). 2011. "Big, Little, Tall, and Tiny: Words That Promote Important Spatial Skills." November 9. www.nsf.gov/news/news_summ.jsp?cntn _id=122226.

Over, H., & M. Carpenter. 2015. "Children Infer Affiliative and Status Relations from Watching Others Imitate." *Developmental Science* 18 (6): 917–25. https://doi.org/10.1111 /desc.12275.

Owen, M.T., J.F. Klausli, A. Mata-Otero, & M. O'Brien Caughy. 2008. "Relationship-Focused Child Care Practices: Quality of Care and Child Outcomes for Children in Poverty." *Early Education and Development* 19 (2): 302–29. https://doi.org/10.1080/10409280801964010.

Page, J. 2018a. "Characterizing the Principles of Professional Love in Early Childhood Care and Education." *International Journal of Early Years Education* 26 (2): 125–41. https://doi.org/10.1080/09669760.2018 .1459508.

Page, J. 2018b. "Love, Care and Intimacy in Early Childhood Education and Care." *International Journal of Early Years Education* 26 (2): 123–24. https://doi.org/10.1080/09669760 .2018.1459509.

Pallini, S., M. Morelli, A. Chirumbolo, R. Baiocco, F. Laghi, & N. Eisenberg. 2019. "Attachment and Attention Problems: A Meta-analysis." *Clinical Psychology Review* 74, 101772. https://doi.org/10.1016/j.cpr.2019.101772

Panfile, T.M., & D.J. Laible. 2012. "Attachment Security and Child's Empathy: The Mediating Role of Emotion Regulation." *Merrill-Palmer Quarterly* 58 (1): 1–21. https://doi.org /10.1353/mpq.2012.0003.

Parlakian, R., & C. Lerner. 2016. "Beyond Twinkle, Twinkle: Using Music with Infants and Toddlers." ZERO TO THREE, August 11. www.zerotothree.org/resources/1514-beyond -twinkle-twinkle-using-music-with-infants -and-toddlers.

Parten, M.B. 1932. "Social Participation Among Preschool Children." *Journal of Abnormal and Social Psychology* 27 (3): 243–69. https://doi .org/10.1037/h0074524.

Peltola, M.J., L. Forssman, K. Puura, M.H. van IJzendoorn, & J.M. Leppänen. 2015. "Attention to Faces Expressing Negative Emotion at 7 Months Predicts Attachment Security at 14 Months." *Child Development* 86 (5): 1321–1332. https://doi.org/10 .1111/cdev.12380.

Petersen, A.C., J. Joseph, & M. Feit, eds. 2014. *New Directions in Child Abuse and Neglect Research*. Washington, DC: National Academies Press.

Piaget, J. 1954. *The Construction of Reality in the Child*. New York: Basic Books.

Piaget, J. 1968. *Six Psychological Studies*. trans. A. Tenzer. New York: Vintage Books.

Porter, P. n.d. "Social Relationships of Infants in Daycare." Accessed February 21, 2019. www.educarer.org/current-article -relationships.htm.

Posada, G., T. Lu, J. Trumbell, G. Kaloustian, M. Trudel, S.J. Plata, P. Peña, J. Perez, S. Tereno, R. Dugravier, G. Coppola, A. Constantini, R. Cassibba, K. Kondo-Ikemura, M. Nóblega, I.M. Haya, C. Pedraglio, M. Verissimo, A.J. Santos, L. Monteiro, & K.L. Lay. 2013. "Is the Secure Base Phenomenon Evident Here, There, and Anywhere? A Cross-Cultural Study of Child Behavior and Experts' Definitions." *Child Development* 84 (6): 1896–905.

Poulin-Dubois, D., E. Bialystok, A. Blaye, A. Polonia, & J. Yott. 2013. "Lexical Access and Vocabulary Development in Very Young Bilinguals." *International Journal of Bilingualism* 17 (1): 57–70. https://doi .org/10.1177/1367006911431198.

Quann, V., & C.A. Wien. 2006. "The Visible Empathy of Infants and Toddlers." *Young Children* 61 (4): 22–29.

Raby, K.L., G.I. Roisman, M.H. Labella, J. Martin, R.C. Fraley, & J.A. Simpson. 2018. "The Legacy of Early Abuse and Neglect for Social and Academic Competence from Childhood to Adulthood." *Child Development*. https://doi .org/10.1111/cdev.13033.

Raikes, H. 1993. "Relationship Duration in Infant Care: Time with a High-Ability Teacher and Infant–Teacher Attachment." *Early Childhood Research Quarterly* 8 (3): 309–325. https://doi.org/10.1016 /S0885-2006(05)80070-5.

Ramírez-Esparza, N., A. García-Sierra, & P.K. Kuhl. 2014. "Look Who's Talking: Speech Style and Social Context in Language Input to Infants are Linked to Concurrent and Future Speech Development." *Developmental Science* 17 (6): 880–91. https://doi.org/10.1111 /desc.12172.

Recchia, S.L., M. Shin, & C. Snaider. 2018. "Where Is the Love? Developing Loving Relationship as an Essential Component of Professional Infant Care." *International Journal of Early Years Education* 26 (2): 142–58. https://doi.org/10.1080/09669760 .2018.1461614.

Reggio Emilia. n.d. "The Environment as the Third Teacher." Accessed March 13, 2019. www.reggioemilia2015.weebly.com /environment-as-a-third-teacher.html.

Repacholi, B.M., & A. Gopnik. 1997. "Early Reasoning About Desires: Evidence from 14- and 18-Month-Olds." *Developmental Psychology* 33 (1): 12–21. https://doi.org /10.1037/0012-1649.33.1.12.

Rhee, S.H., N.P. Friedman, D.L. Boeldt, R.P. Corley, J.K. Hewitt, A. Knafo, B.B. Lahey, J.A. Robinson, C.A. Van Hulle, I.D. Waldman, S.E. Young, & C. Zahn-Waxler. 2013. "Early Concern and Disregard for Others as Predictors of Antisocial Behavior." *Journal of Child Psychology and Psychiatry* 54 (2): 157–166. https://doi.org/10.1111/j.1469 -7610.2012.02574.x.

Rhyner, P.M., K.L. Guenther, K. Pizur-Barnekow, S.E. Cashin, & A.L. Chavie. 2012. "Child Caregivers' Contingent Responsiveness Behaviors During Interactions With Toddlers Within Three Day Care Contexts." *Communications Disorders Quarterly* 34 (4): 232–41. https://doi .org/10.1177/1525740112465174.

Rinaldi, C. 1994. "Staff Development in Reggio Emilia." In *Reflections on the Reggio Emilia Approach. Perspectives from ERIC/EECE,* A Monograph Series No. 6, eds. L.G. Katz & B. Cesarone, 55–60. Urbana, IL: ERIC Clearinghouse on Elementary and Early Childhood Education.

Rochat, P. 2003. "Five Levels of Self-Awareness as They Unfold Early in Life." *Consciousness and Cognition* 12 (4): 717–31. https://doi. org.10.1016/S1053-8100(03)00081-3.

Rokita, K.I., M.R. Dauvermann, & G. Donohoe. 2018. "Early Life Experiences and Social Cognition in Major Psychiatric Disorders: A Systematic Review." *European Psychiatry* 53: 123–33. https://doi.org/10.1016/j. eurpsy.2018.06.006.

Ross, J., D. Martin, & S. Cunningham. 2016. "How Do Children Develop a Sense of Self?" *The Conversation,* October 17. www.theconversation.com/how-do-children -develop-a-sense-of-self-56118.

Roth-Hanania, R., M. Davidov, & C. Zahn-Waxler. 2011. "Empathy Development from 8 to 16 Months: Early Signs of Concern for Others." *Infant Behavior & Development* 34 (3): 447–58. https://doi.org/10.1016/j.infbeh .2011.04.007.

Rothman, J. 2014. "The Meaning of 'Culture.'" *The New Yorker.* December 26. www .newyorker.com/books/joshua-rothman /meaning-culture.

Rouse, E., & F. Hadley. 2018. "Where Did Love and Care Get Lost? Educators and Parents' Perceptions of Early Childhood Practice." *International Journal of Early Years Education* 26 (2): 159–72. https://doi.org /10.1080/09669760.2018.1461613.

Rubin, K.H., K.B. Burgess, & P.D. Hastings. 2002. "Stability and Social-Behavioral Consequences of Toddlers' Inhibited Temperament and Parenting Behaviors." *Child Development* 73 (2): 483–95. https://doi.org/10.1111 /1467-8624.00419.

Ruprecht, K., J. Elicker, & J.Y. Choi. 2016. "Continuity of Care, Caregiver–Child Interactions, and Toddler Social Competence and Problem Behaviors." *Early Education and Development* 27 (2): 221–39. https://doi.org /10.1080/10409289.2016.1102034.

Ryan, S.M., & T.H. Ollendick. 2018. "The Interaction Between Child Behavioral Inhibition and Parenting Behaviors: Effects on Internalizing and Externalizing Symptomology." *Clinical Child Family Psychology Review* 21 (3): 320–39. https:// doi.org/10.1007/s10567-018-0254-9.

Saylor, M.M., P.A. Ganea, & M.D. Vázquez. 2011. "What's Mine Is Mine: Twelve-Month-Olds Use Possessive Pronouns to Identify Referents." *Developmental Science* 14 (4): 859–64. https://doi.org/10.1111/j.1467-7687 .2010.01034.x.

Schulz, L. 2015. "Infants Explore the Unexpected." *Science* 348 (6230): 42–43. https://doi.org /10.1126/science.aab0582.

Schuhmacher, N., M. Köster, & J. Kärtner. 2018. "Modeling Prosocial Behavior Increases Helping in 16-Month-Olds." *Child Development* 90 (5): 1789–801. https://doi.org/10.1111/cdev.13054.

Sciaraffa, M. A., P.D. Zeanah, & C.H. Zeanah. 2018. "Understanding and Promoting Resilience in the Context of Adverse Childhood Experiences." *Early Childhood Education Journal* 46 (3): 343–53. doi:10.1007/s10643-017-0869-3

Seal, B.C., & R.A. Depaolis. 2014. "Manual Activity and Onset of First Words in Babies Exposed and Not Exposed to Baby Signing." *Sign Language Studies* 14 (4): 444–65. https://doi.org/10.1353/sls.2014.0015.

Seitz, H. 2008. "The Power of Documentation in the Early Childhood Classroom." *Young Children* 63 (2): 88–93. www.naeyc.org/sites/default/files/globally-shared/downloads/PDFs/resources/pubs/seitz.pdf.

Shai, D., & J. Belsky. 2017. "Parental Embodied Mentalizing: How the Nonverbal Dance Between Parents and Infants Predicts Children's Socio–Emotional Functioning." *Attachment & Human Development* 19 (2): 191–219. https://doi.org/10.1080/14616734.2016.1255653.

Shin, M. 2010. "Peeking at the Relationship World of Infant Friends and Caregivers." *Journal of Early Childhood Research* 8 (3): 294–302. https://doi.org/10.1177/1476718X10366777.

Shin, M., & T. Partyka. 2017. "Empowering Infants Through Responsive and Intentional Play Activities." *International Journal of Early Years Education* 25 (2): 127–142. https://doi.org/10.1080/09669760.2017.1291331.

Sosinsky, L., K. Ruprecht, D. Horm, K. Kriener-Althen, C. Vogel, & T. Halle. 2016. *Including Relationship-Based Care Practices in Infant–Toddler Care: Implications for Practice and Policy*. OPRE # 2016-46. Washington, DC: OPRE. www.acf.hhs.gov/sites/default/files/opre/nitr_inquire_may_2016_070616_b508compliant.pdf.

Stahl, A.E., & L. Feigenson. 2015. "Observing the Unexpected Enhances Infants' Learning and Exploration." *Science* 248 (6230): 91–94. https://doi.org/10.1126/science.aaa3799.

Stahl, A.E., & L. Feigenson. 2017. "Expectancy Violations Promote Learning in Young Children." *Cognition* 163: 1–14. https://doi.org/10.1016/j.cognition.2017.02.008.

Stern, J.A., J.L. Borelli, & P.A. Smiley. 2015. "Assessing Parental Empathy: A Role for Empathy in Child Attachment." *Attachment & Human Development* 17 (1): 1–22. https://doi.org/10.1080/14616734.2014.969749.

Stifter, C.A., S. Putnam, & L. Jahromi. 2008. "Exuberant and Inhibited Toddlers: Stability of Temperament and Risk for Problem Behavior." *Development and Psychopathology* 20 (2): 401–21. doi.org/10.1017/S0954579408000199.

Tamis-LeMonda, C.S., Y. Kuchirko, & L. Song. 2014. "Why Is Infant Language Learning Facilitated by Parental Responsiveness?" *Current Directions in Psychological Science* 23 (2): 121–26. https://doi.org/10.1177/0963721414522813.

Tayler, C. 2015. "Learning in Early Childhood: Experiences, Relationships, and 'Learning to Be.'" *European Journal of Education* 50 (2): 160–74. https://doi.org/10.1111/ejed.12117.

Thomas, A., & S. Chess. 1977. *Temperament and Development*. New York: Brunner/Mazel.

Thomason, A.C., & K.M. La Paro. 2013. "Teachers' Commitment to the Field and Teacher–Child Interactions in Center-Based Child Care for Toddlers and Three-Year-Olds." *Early Childhood Education Journal* 41 (3): 227–34. https://doi.org/10.1007/s10643-012-0539-4.

Tronick, E. 2007. *The Neurobehavioral and Social-Emotional Development of Infants and Children*. New York: W.W. Norton.

Ulber, J., K. Hamann, & M. Tomasello. 2015. "How 18- and 24-Month-Old Peers Divide Resources Among Themselves." *Journal of Experimental Child Psychology* 140: 228–44. https://doi.org/10.1016/j.jecp.2015.07.009.

Van Berkel, S. R., M.G. Groeneveld, J. Mesman, J.J. Endendijk, E.T. Hallers-Haalboom, L.D. van der Pol, & M.J. Bakermans-Kranenburg. 2015. "Parental Sensitivity Towards Toddlers and Infant Siblings Predicting Toddler Sharing and Compliance." *Journal of Child and Family Studies* 24 (8): 2270–2279. https://doi.org/10.1007/s10826-014-0029-y.

Vaughn, B.E., T.E.A. Waters, R.D. Steele, G.I. Roisman, K.K. Bost, W. Truitt, H. Waters, & C. Booth-Laforce. 2016. "Multiple Domains of Parental Secure Base Support During Childhood and Adolescence Contribute to Adolescents' Representations of Attachment as a Secure Base Script." *Attachment & Human Development* 18 (4): 317–36. doi:10.1080 /14616734.2016.1162180.

Verdine, B.N., R.M. Golinkoff, K. Hirsh-Pasek, N.S. Newcombe, A.T. Filipowicz, & A. Chang. 2014. "Deconstructing Building Blocks: Preschoolers' Spatial Assembly Performance Relates to Early Mathematical Skills." *Child Development* 85 (3): 1062–1076. https://doi .org/10.1111/cdev.12165.

Vygotsky, L.S. 1978. *Mind in Society: The Development of Higher Psychological Processes.* Eds. M. Cole, V. John-Steiner, S. Scribner, & E. Souberman. Cambridge, MA: Harvard University Press. http://ouleft.org/wp-content /uploads/Vygotsky-Mind-in-Society.pdf.

Whitehurst, G.J., F.L. Falco, C.J. Lonigan, J.E. Fischel, B.D. DeBaryshe, M.C. Valdez-Menchaca, & M. Caulfield. 1988. "Accelerating Language Development Through Picture Book Reading." *Development Psychology* 24 (4): 552–59. https://doi.org/10.1037/0012-1649 .24.4.552.

Wittmer, D.S., & D.W. Clauson. 2018. *From Biting to Hugging: Understanding Social Development in Infants and Toddlers.* Lewisville, NC: Gryphon House.

Wittmer, D.S., & A.S. Honig. 1991. "Convergent or Divergent? Teacher Questions to Three-Year-Old Children in Day Care." *Early Child Development and Care* 68 (1): 141–47.

Wittmer, D.S., & S.H. Petersen. 2018. *Infant and Toddler Development and Responsive Program Planning: A Relationship-Based Approach.* 4th ed. New York: Pearson.

Yeary, J. 2018. "Rocking and Rolling. The Calm in the Storm: Supporting Young Children Before, During, and After a Community Disaster or Trauma." *Young Children* 73 (5): 84–92. www.naeyc.org/resources/pubs /yc/nov2018/supporting-young-children -community-disaster.

Yu, C., & L.B. Smith. 2016. "The Social Origins of Sustained Attention in One-Year-Old Human Infants." *Current Biology* 26 (9): 1235–40. https://doi.org/10.1016/j.cub.2016.03.026.

ZERO TO THREE. n.d. "The Expectation Gap." Accessed March 13, 2019. https:// www.zerotothree.org/resources/series/the -expectation-gap.

Zysset, A.E., T.H. Kakebeeke, N. Messerli–Bürgy, A.H. Meyer, K. Stülb, C.S. Leeger-Aschmann, E.A. Schmutz, A. Arhab, J.J. Puder, S. Kriemler, S. Munsch, & O.G. Jenni. 2018. "Predictors of Executive Functions in Preschoolers: Findings from the SPLASHY Study." *Frontiers in Psychology* 9 (2060): 1–11. https://doi .org/10.3389/fpsyg.2018.02060.

Acknowledgments

I dedicate this book to my husband, children, and grandchildren who inspire me each day to live life wholeheartedly. I thank Dr. Alice Honig for authoring this book with me. She is my mentor, coauthor, and friend. I thank those who have led the way in the vitally important field of infant and toddler development—Alice Honig, Ron Lally, Peter Mangione, and many others. They have motivated me to continually strive to improve the lives of infants and toddlers and their families and teachers. I thank Holly Bohart at NAEYC for making this book a possibility and improving its quality. I also dedicate this book to you—the readers—who know that the career of supporting the development and learning of infants and toddlers is one of the most important professional callings that exists. My hope is that each day you will enjoy responsive, caring, and compassionate relationships with infants and toddlers. Young children need care and learning programs that are created to be day to day the relationship way. I would like to acknowledge the importance of NAEYC in my professional life in early childhood education. From the beginning of my career 50 years ago, NAEYC has provided the inspiration, knowledge, and vision of quality that has motivated me to focus on improving programs for children, teachers, and administrators. I have attended many NAEYC conferences and used many of its excellent resources. This organization has been a guiding light that leads myself and others to improve educational and life opportunities for young children and those who care for them. I feel honored to write this book on how to provide responsive, relationship-based programs for infants and toddlers.

—Donna S. Wittmer

I am grateful for this opportunity to thank all those who have made possible my career in human development and lifetime devotion to celebrate, study, write about, work with, and serve families and young children and their caregivers. For decades, my goal has been to enhance and encourage children's flourishing and resilience to master new learnings and to have courage to cope with life's difficulties and celebrate life's joys. I learned first from my own children, Lawrence Honig, Madeleine Lenski, and Jonathan Honig, to develop more patience and more insight and respect for each child's special gifts, passions, temperament, and emotional needs. I have also been privileged to learn from my nine grandchildren how to honor the unique pathways each child journeys to serve others and to forge loving and caring relationships in their lives. I am deeply grateful for all the children and parents whom I have been privileged to work with in my private practice as a licensed psychotherapist. I shall always be grateful to my graduate students who I admire so deeply for their perseverance and striving for wisdom in their studies of child development. I am forever indebted to my mentor, Dr. Bettye Caldwell, of blessed memory, who gave me my first job as Research Assistant and later the responsibility of training staff for her visionary pioneer founding of the Children's Center serving infants and toddlers in Syracuse, New York.

—Alice S. Honig

About the Authors

Donna S. Wittmer received her PhD from Syracuse University. She taught behavioral pediatrics at Upstate Medical Center and also provided early intervention assessment and intervention services on the Onondaga Indian Nation. She was a professor of early childhood/early childhood special education at the University of Colorado Denver for 17 years. Donna is a fellow of Zero to Three.

Donna coauthored *Infant and Toddler Development and Responsive Program Planning* (4th ed.), *Endless Possibilities,* (2nd ed.), and *The Young Child from Birth to 8* (7th ed.). Her most recent books include *From Biting to Hugging—Understanding Social Development in Infants and Toddlers* and *Crying and Laughing—Understanding the Emotional Development of Infants and Toddlers.* She is the author of numerous articles on early childhood education and has presented at many NAEYC and Zero to Three conferences.

Alice Sterling Honig, PhD, is professor emerita of child development at Syracuse University, where for 36 years she directed the annual National Quality Infant/Toddler Caregiving Workshop. She received the university's highest honor, the Chancellor's Citation for Exceptional Academic Achievement.

Dr. Honig has published 600 articles and book chapters, more than two dozen books, and several videos for parents and caregivers. She served as Research in Review editor for NAEYC's peer-reviewed journal, *Young Children,* for six years and has lectured widely in the United States and abroad.

Dr. Honig was program director of the Children's Center, a pioneer enrichment project serving infants and young children and their families in Syracuse. As a volunteer she led sessions for the Onondaga County Mental Health Association to help parents with difficult divorce and custody issues. In 2013 she presented the first Dr. Alice Honig award in China to a prominent Beijing pediatrician. In 2015 Dr. Bettye Caldwell endowed an undergraduate Falk College scholarship in Dr. Honig's name.

Check Out These High-Quality Resources

THIS IS **naeyc**
PLAY

Environments and Interactions that
Engage Infants and Toddlers

Julia Luckenbill, Aarti Subramaniam,
& Janet Thompson

Browse Our Collection
NAEYC.org

Families &
Educators
Together

Building Great Relationships
that Support Young Children

Derry Koralek, Karen Nemeth,
& Kelly Ramsey

Spotlight on Young Children

Russella Procaccio and
Holly Bohart, editors

Social and Emotional
Development

naeyc
THE ESSENTIALS

**Providing High-Quality
Family Child Care**

Marie L. Masterson and Lisa M. Ginet

Foreword by Bill Hudson

Developmentally
Appropriate Practice:
Focus on
Infants
and Toddlers

Carol Copple, Sue Bredekamp,
Derry Koralek, and Kathy Charner, editors

naeyc